Encouragement

For overcoming life's challenges

Ernest Tobar

Lessons Learned From The Book Of Life

This book is dedicated to

All those who have been an encouragement to my life

Pastor Randy Meeks

who believed in my ministry of teaching and gave me a platform

Pernell Hill

whose example as an author and speaker inspired me to write a book

My Wife

who has stood by my side and believed in my gifts and talents

To family and great friends

who have all been there to encourage and speak into my life

To our Lord who deserves all the praise and glory who has changed my destiny forever

Hardcover: 979-8-218-99576-8

Paperback: 979-8-218-99577-5

eBook: 979-8-218-99575-1

Book Cover By: Ernest Tobar & Pernell Hill

Published By: Ernest Tobar

Formatted, Marketed, and Powered By: DHK Creations & Publications, LLC

Table Of Contents

Introduction

It is my desire that this book encourages you in your time of need. We all face challenges in life, some more difficult than others. Hopefully somewhere in the pages of this book you will find a truth, an example, scripture that will encourage you to go on in spite of your difficulties and challenges.

Just some background on my life. I was the oldest of six children, three brothers and two sisters. We were a close-knit family, struggled financially but all our needs were met. My father was a hard worker who instilled into me and my three brothers a strong work ethic. My mother was the glue that held our family together who in her own way taught me the power of faith. The doctors told her she would never have children. She wanted kids and a family so she prayed and ask God for a miracle and here all six of us came into the world. It was a non-Christian family but we were taught respect, enduring love and forgiveness. Yet because of not having the covering of a church and we were all unsaved we all fell captive into various bondages, sins and much despair and discouragement.

The day came when at the age of 16 I began to search to fill the emptiness, daily discouragement and lack of real purpose in my life. It was at the age of 17, I met a young man name Wayne

Tyllich who invited me to a church called Lindale Assembly of God. It forever changed my destiny and I will always be grateful. That invitation to church and later accepting Jesus as Lord and Savior not only effected my life but it effected my whole family that in time every one of them were changed.

The saving grace of Jesus is one of the greatest life changing experiences that can fill an empty life with peace, love and divine purpose and encouragement in life and in the life to come.

So be encouraged as you read this book, knowing that the greatest encourager in life is our Lord Jesus who defeated the greatest discourager in life Satan and who causes us to triumph in life's challenges.

Additional Notes:

Greek definitions are taken from Online Bible Hub

Quotes of various individuals are italicized

Commentaries used were Matthew Henry, Benson and Barnes

All Bible verses, unless otherwise indicated, are King James Version

CHAPTER 1

According To Your Faith

(MATTHEW 9:29)

Introduction

The longer I live as a Christian, the more I realize the importance of one single trait that's vital to our lives. This trait is vital to answered prayers, to failure or success, and having either a cynical or positive outlook on life. It is vital to loving or avoiding difficult people, surviving in difficult circumstances, the list can go on and on. What is that exactly? It is the truth about Jesus. While He walked among men and women He encouraged it in others.

He admired it in others and responded to it in others, it was **faith** in Him. If we meet certain conditions such as forgiving others and not having sin in our lives, the Lord Jesus has promised to answer according to our faith. The Greek word for faith is **pistis** it means *a firm persuasion*, a conviction based upon hearing of God's word. Webster defines it as *confidence, belief, unquestioning belief in God.* It is complete trust and reliance.

Reading of Various Scriptures on Faith

The Blind Men's Faith of Desperation — Matthew 9:27-30

And when Jesus departed thence, two blind men followed him, crying, and saying, Thou son of David, have mercy on us. 28And when he was come into the house, the blind men came to him: and Jesus saith unto them, Believe ye that I am able to do this? They said unto him, Yea, Lord. 29 Then touched he their eyes, saying, According to your faith be it unto you. 30And their eyes were opened; and Jesus straitly charged them, saying, See that no man know it.

When they begged for a cure, he inquired into their faith (v. 28), "Believe ye that I am able?" He did not inquire into their wealth, whether they were able to pay him for a cure; nor into their reputation, should he get credit by curing them; but into their faith. Can you imagine what it must have been like to not have sight, and then your eyes are opened, and the first person you see is Jesus? I imagine this being their experience. Can you imagine the emotions of joy and gratefulness they felt as they beheld the Son of God? Jesus' actions said, "I know you believe, and the power you believe in, shall be given to you; according to your faith, be it unto you."

The Woman Who Touched the Hem of Jesus Garment in secret — Matthew 9:20-22

20 Just then a woman who had been subject to bleeding for

twelve years came up behind him and touched the edge of his cloak. ²¹ She said to herself, "If I only touch his cloak, I will be healed." ²² Jesus turned and saw her. "Take heart, daughter," he said, "your faith has healed you." And the woman was healed at that moment.

Comment: Notice her real, but imperfect faith. There was unquestionable confidence in Christ's power, and a very genuine desire for healing. But it was a very simple faith. She believes that her touch of the garment will heal without Christ's will or knowledge, and she could just take the healing and run off into the crowd. This is not the case, Jesus asks who touched me? He sensed virtue or power flow out of Him. It is like people who pray and pray doubting their prayers will be answered or in this case many who touched Him but only one touched with true heartfelt faith, and immediately He responds to her.

The Centurion who Recognized and Believed in Jesus Authority — Matt. 8:5-13

When Jesus had entered Capernaum, a centurion came to him, asking for help. ⁶ "Lord," he said, "my servant lies at home paralyzed, suffering terribly." ⁷ Jesus said to him, "Shall I come and heal him?" ⁸ The centurion replied, "Lord, I do not deserve to have you come under my roof. But just say the word, and my servant will be healed. ⁹ For I myself am a man under authority, with soldiers under me. I tell this one, 'Go,' and he goes; and that one, 'Come,' and he comes. I say to my servant, 'Do this,' and he does it." ¹⁰ When Jesus heard this, he was amazed and said to those following him, "Truly I tell you, I have not found anyone in Israel with such great faith. [11] I say to you that many will come from the east and the west, and will take their places at the feast with Abraham, Isaac and Jacob in the kingdom of heaven. [12] But the subjects of the kingdom will be thrown outside, into the darkness, where there will be weeping and gnashing of teeth." [13] Then Jesus said to the centurion, "Go! Let it be done just as you believed it would." And his servant was healed at that moment.

Comment: This centurion was a Roman soldier. Though he was a soldier, yet he was a godly man. No man's calling or place is an excuse for unbelief and sin. See how he states his servant's case in humility and in love for his servant. Here the centurion sees Jesus to have Divine power, and a full command of all the creatures and powers of nature, even as a master over his servants. Such servants we all should be to God; we must go and come, according to the directions of his word and the disposals of his providence.

But when the Son of man comes he finds little faith, therefore he finds little fruit. An outward profession may cause us to be called children of the kingdom; but if we rest in just that, and have nothing else to show, we shall be cast out. The servant got cured of his disease, and the master got the approval of his faith. What was said to him, is said to all, Believe, and ye shall receive; only believe. See the power of Christ, and the power of faith.

Examples of Personal Faith

I still remember the seven months of unemployment and

temporary jobs, my wife's battle with cancer and then having to fight back discouragement. I did this by encouraging myself in how Jesus had given grace and strength and answered prayers in the past. I encouraged myself in the words of Jesus in Luke 18:1 — "that men should always pray and not faint. I listened to Christian music, prayed with other believers. When some would ask if I had found a job, I would say in faith the job is coming. Keeping faith in the Lord and His word was the only way to survive and overcome discouragement.

There is a term in exercising that is called point of failure. For muscles to grow stronger you must exercise them until your muscle cannot make another movement. If you just exercise enough where it is comfortable you will just maintain, but when you push harder, they will grow stronger. It is the same way in our spiritual walk where we endure to the point of failure and then the Lord steps in by His Holy Spirit gives us His rest and strength and causes our faith to go from the point of failure to stronger faith in Him. Maybe you are at that point of failure, now is not the time to quit but the time to keep your faith in Jesus and He will intervene in your life.

Conclusion

The word of God encourages us in Hebrews 10:35-36 *So do not throw away your confidence; it will be richly rewarded. 36 You need to persevere so that when you have done the will of God, you will receive what he has promised.* Remember we have eternal promises, and present day promises in this life. What are you believing in

God for? Let's remember the words of Jesus who said to various people in different walks of life, according to your faith be it done unto you.

CHAPTER 2

Are You At The Breaking Point In Your Life

(PSALM 68:19)

Introduction

There will be times in our lives where we feel we have reached the breaking point in our lives. It plays no favorites; it can affect celebrities down to the common everyday working men and women of our society as well as the young and the aged. God's word in *Psalm 68:19 says, "Praise be to the LORD, to God our Savior, who daily bears our burdens."* When we allow the Lord to carry our burdens, He can supernaturally ease the breaking points in our lives.

Definition of Breaking Point

In human psychology, *the breaking point is a moment of stress in which a person breaks down or a situation becomes critical.* The intensity of environmental stress necessary to bring this about varies from individual to individual. If something or someone has reached breaking point, they have so many problems or difficulties that they can no longer cope with them and may soon collapse or be unable to continue. The point at which physical, mental, or emotional strength gives way under stress. The point at which a condition or situation becomes critical.

Modern Day Examples of People Reaching Their Breaking Point

There is a story of an Arizona physician who retired after 37-year practice... He says everything has just turned into a giant paperwork mill with all the government regulations. He said the government had pushed him to the breaking point.

Other times it can be a tragedy. NFL star Danny 'DJ' Ware spoke of the tragic death of his three-year-old son who was killed while riding his bicycle. Danny said, "my life has been a roller coaster." He said "please pray for my family as I am at a breaking point."

There are various areas of life where people reach their breaking point. For example, worrying about a loved one, a struggling son, a daughter, a sick relative whose condition is terminal. Financial struggles as a single parent can be mental torture. A work situation has you on pins and needles with layoffs looming. Maybe it is postpartum depression, or various health issues. These are just several examples of how one can reach their breaking point.

Stories from scriptures of those who experienced God's spiritual strength and grace to continue:

Mary and Martha (Luke 10:41-42) "Martha, Martha," the Lord answered, "you are worried and upset about many things, [42] but few things are needed — or indeed only one. Mary has chosen what is better, and it will not be taken away from her."

Martha, like us, knew Jesus, and wanted to serve Him well. But she was so busy serving Him that she didn't have time to listen to Him, and Jesus corrected her for that. We need to listen well when Jesus corrects us and gives us His insight. Jesus told Martha that Mary had chosen what was better and that was to sit at His feet and listen to His word. Prayer and meditating on the word have a peaceful calming effect upon our lives. He knows how to order our lives and how we can be refueled and refreshed by planning a daily time and maybe times during the day in His presence and word. **It can bring a Mary moment into our Martha lives.**

Story of Cornelius the Roman Centurion

God desires to lead us into a greater revelation and relationship with Him resulting in our Salvation regardless of circumstances.

Acts 10:2-5, A devout man, and one that feared God with all his house, which gave many alms to the people, and prayed to God always. 3 He saw in a vision evidently about the ninth hour of the day an angel of God coming in to him, and saying unto him, Cornelius. 4 And when he looked on him, he was afraid, and said, What is it, Lord? And he said unto him, Thy prayers and thine alms are come up for a memorial before God. 5 And now send men to Joppa, and call for one Simon, whose surname is Peter:

Acts 10:30-36, And Cornelius said, Four days ago I was fasting until this hour; and at the ninth hour I prayed in my house, and, behold, a man stood before me in bright clothing, 31 And said,

Cornelius, thy prayer is heard, and thine alms are had in remembrance in the sight of God.

³² Send therefore to Joppa, and call hither Simon, whose surname is Peter; he is lodged in the house of one Simon a tanner by the seaside: who, when he cometh, shall speak unto thee. ³³ Immediately therefore I sent to thee; and thou hast well done that thou art come. Now therefore are we all here present before God, to hear all things that are commanded thee of God. ³⁴ Then Peter opened his mouth, and said, Of a truth I perceive that God is no respecter of persons: ³⁵ But in every nation he that feareth him, and worketh righteousness, is accepted with him. ³⁶The word which God sent unto the children of Israel, preaching peace by Jesus Christ: (he is Lord of all:)

Cornelius was a Roman centurion who was a military leader occupying a nation who did not want him in Judea. He was trying to raise a family, wanting to help the poor and was concerned about his spiritual condition, because he realized he needed more. He is struggling with it all, until he hears Peter explain about Jesus dying for the sins of the world. Cornelius, his family and his friends find a new life in Christ, are filled with the Spirit and baptized in the name of Jesus. His circumstances did not change but knowing Jesus gave Him a power and spiritual awakening, something he did not have, before knowing Christ.

Story of Moses and Jethro His Father-in-Law

Being willing to take corrections even from an unlikely source, can relieve a lot of stress and keep us from a breaking point. **Exodus**

18:15-18, [15] And Moses said to his father-in-law, "Because the people come to me to inquire of God; [16] when they have a dispute, they come to me and I decide between one person and another, and I make them know the statutes of God and his laws." [17] Moses' father-in-law said to him, "What you are doing is not good. [18] You and the people with you will certainly wear yourselves out, for the thing is too heavy for you. You are not able to do it alone.

There are times we are taking on too much, we must reorganize and be open to other suggestions of doing things in a better way as Jethro Moses' father-in-law did. In Exodus 18 we see Moses beginning in the morning until evening trying to solve everyone's disputes. Jethro saw this and pulled him to the side and said to paraphrase "this was not a good thing." He said that this would eventually wear Moses out and suggests he pick out good God-fearing men to handle many of the disputes and Moses would handle the more difficult ones.

That's what we need to do, get organized, clear the clutter, for it is easier to be productive when we do. In heaven, God is organized. God's angels, His works, His whole creation is organized. Just take the time, be open to suggestions, and do it today, don't procrastinate. You will have more time, and less stress in the future.

Simplify Your Life, follow the Pattern of Jesus

Acts 10:38-39, [38] how God anointed Jesus of Nazareth with the Holy Spirit and with power. He went about doing good and healing all who were oppressed by the devil, for God was with him.

[39] And we are witnesses of all that he did both in the country of the Jews and in Jerusalem.

Did you notice, Jesus did not go around doing everything? He went around doing good and He did it within three years. Before Jesus came, Israel was filled with people who were sick, blind, deaf, lame, demon oppressed and possessed and lost. He came to do not His will but the will of God the Father and to glorify Him on the earth. In John 17:4 He said, 'I have glorified You on the earth. I have finished the work which you have given me to do.

God does not expect us to do everything, but the tasks He has assigned us we must do them well and let others take care of other tasks, and leave the results to Him. We are not serving ministry, but the Lord of the ministry.

Practical Applications

A. Life will not work right until we first receive Him as Savior like Cornelius the Roman centurion.

B. Sit at His feet like Mary and we will experience His peace and presence.

C. Be open to suggestions on better managing our tasks like Moses, this can relieve much tension.

D. Live a simpler lifestyle after the pattern of Jesus. This will bring us into His peace.

Conclusion

We need to trust God and His word and get into His presence every day. We need to take charge of our day by letting Him take charge of us every day. He specializes in handling the day-to-day issues in our lives as we turn those to Him. He is the expert at handling impossible days and making them productive days. It is then that our breaking points can be the starting points for His grace and power to take over in our lives and He will be glorified and lifted, and He will draw men to Himself.

CHAPTER 3

Where Is Your Confidence

(HEBREWS 10:35)

Introduction

Where is your confidence when you lose your job, when your health fails, your children go astray, when your dog runs away. When all else fails and our confidence is in the Lord, He will cause us to overcome in life. In this study we will look at the importance of keeping our confidence in God's powerful promises when facing life's difficulties.

Definition of Confidence

Hebrew Definition — From batach; a refuge, i.e. (objective) security, or assurance — (subjective) confidence, hope, sure, trust.

Greek Definition — parrhńsía (from pás, "all" and rhńsis, "a proverb or statement quoted with resolve," — (bold resolve). freedom, openness, especially in speech; boldness.

Webster's Definition — a feeling or belief that you can do something well or succeed at something.: a feeling or belief that someone or something is good or can succeed at something.: the feeling of being certain that something will happen or that something is true.

Reading of Hebrews 10:32-37

[32] But remember the former days, when, after being enlightened, you endured a great conflict of sufferings, [33] partly by being made a public spectacle through reproaches and tribulations, and partly by becoming sharers with those who were so treated. [34] You sympathized with those in prison and joyfully accepted the confiscation of your property, knowing that you yourselves had a better and permanent possession. [35] So do not throw away your confidence; it holds a great reward. [36] You need to persevere, so that after you have done God's will, you will receive what He has promised [37] For yet in a very little while, He who is coming will come and will not delay.

Commentary Matthew Henry

Many and various afflictions united against the early Christians, and they had a great conflict. The Christian spirit is not a selfish spirit; it puts us upon pitying others, visiting them, helping them, and pleading for them. All things here are but shadows. The happiness of the saints in heaven will last forever; enemies can never take it away as earthly goods. This will make rich amends for all we may lose and suffer here. The greatest part of the saints' happiness yet is in promise. It is a trial of the patience of Christians, to be content to live after their work is done, and to stay for their reward till God's time to give comes.

He will soon come to them at death, to end all their sufferings, and to give them a crown of life. The Christian's present conflict may be sharp but will be soon over. God never is pleased with the formal profession and outward duties and services of such as do not persevere; but he beholds them with great displeasure. And those who have been kept faithful in great trials for the time past, have reason to hope for the same grace to help them still to live by faith, till they receive the end of their faith and patience, even the salvation of their souls. Living by faith, and dying in faith, our souls are safe forever.

Comments for discussion on these verses.

The writer of Hebrews exhorts the believers to remember the former days when they were first saved, and how they joyfully endured many trials and afflictions.

As believers we are persecuted at times, we are mocked and ridiculed, along with others. 1st Peter 5:9 notes "Whom we resist steadfast in the faith (Satan), knowing that the same afflictions are being accomplished in your brothers that are in the world."

The Hebrew Christians had pity on those in prison and so should we. Jesus came to set the captives free.

These Hebrew Christians lost some things in this life but did not lose their joy. The book of Hebrews encourages us not to throw away our confidence in the Lord. He has kept us since we first got saved and will keep us to the end.

We need to continue to persevere for He has promised to come back for His own and He does reward perseverance and faith. As believers we should look forward with expectancy and with joy for His return. We will be rewarded for our confidence in Him.

Story of Praying for a family in a Hopeless Situation

I remember some members of my family who had to move because their landlord was selling the house they were living in. As I looked at the situation I felt their hopelessness. The family had physical disabilities, addictions, meager income, a wrecked car and nowhere to go. I prayed with them and in confidence, believing God for His provision. As God heard the prayer He intervened and they found a better house, we helped them with their car repair, and they were able to be settled in a better house. They now own their own home.

Story of King David's Deep Confidence in God

So, what made David different? It was not because he had the self-generated, raw, cool courage of the American action-movie hero. What fueled David's courage was his confidence in God's promises and God's power to fulfill them.

In the preceding chapter, Samuel the prophet had informed David that God had chosen him to be the next king of Israel and anointed him with his brothers around him (1 Samuel 16:13). David knew this information when he arrived in the camp and heard Goliath's sneering rants. And he drew additional confidence by remembering how God had helped him in the past with other challenges (1 Samuel 17:34–36).

David believed that God would never break his promise, and if Goliath made himself an obstacle to God's promise, God could flick him out of the way with a pebble. David saw God as bigger and stronger than the fearful Philistine. So, he went out to fight knowing that God would give him victory over Goliath — and when he did, the victory would demonstrate God's power and faithfulness, not David's courage (1 Samuel 17:46–47).

These giants, who are bigger than we are and very intimidating to our flesh, will be slain just like David's was — by faith. And our courage to face them will not come from our self-confidence, it will only come from confidence in God's powerful promises.

Conclusion

God wants us to live life with a confidence in Him that will cause us to be steadfast in our walk. Confidence will cause us to persevere and move forward in faith when the circumstances are telling us to just quit and give up. Remember, the next time you are facing what seems to be defeat or a great loss or sorrow, that is the very time we need to not throw away our confidence in the Lord for He does in time reward our faith and confidence in Him.

CHAPTER 4

Scriptures To Fight Depression And Hopelessness

Introduction

STOP, DON'T DO IT! Take hope! You have options that you cannot see right now! It is not that you do not have options, it is just that you cannot see them. Evil forces cloud our minds from seeing the hope of a better day. It is coming. Only the word of God can strip away the darkness so that we can see the brightness. You are in the dark simply because you cannot see the light. Hurt and hopelessness work together to block the light. The light is all around you. MAKE YOURSELF read the following scriptures, even if you feel absolutely nothing. The deadness will leave. Hope and light will seep into your heart. Do it!

Depression and suicidal thoughts only survive within an outlook of complete hopelessness. Hope, true Bible hope, is the best antidote for hopelessness. Take the hope that resides in the promises of God and let it dwell in your heart. Your outlook will change. God has a wonderful habit of raising individuals out of impossible situations. He enjoys doing it, and it brings Him glory.

The Bible is filled with stories of people, just like you, that were delivered out of extremely dangerous and potentially embarrassing situations — including His own son, Jesus. You are no different.

Reject the guilt and shame, and absorb His love, forgiveness, and hope. You will make it out of this situation! The darkness will not last. That is the real truth, but for it to work, you must see it as truth and believe it. This is where reading, speaking, and meditating on God's promises comes in. When you do these things, hope and belief will grow in your heart.

Stories of People Who Battled Depression and Overcame

Depression is real, and if you are fighting it, you are not alone. Depression seems to have been the bane of many of life's great leaders. In the Bible, Moses, Elijah, David, and Job all had to deal with it. In the secular world, Sir Winston Churchill used to call depression his 'black dog'.

President Abraham Lincoln battled depression and suicide all his adult life. There were times when for his own safety Lincoln would not allow himself to carry a knife, for fear that he would hurt himself, or worse. Elizabeth Keckley, Mary Lincoln's dressmaker, once told of watching the president drag himself into the room where she was fitting the First Lady. *"His step was slow and heavy, and his face sad,"* Keckley recalled. *"Like a tired child he threw himself upon a sofa and shaded his eyes with his hands. He was a complete picture of dejection."* He had just returned from the War Department, he said, where the news was "dark, dark everywhere.

Lincoln then took a small Bible from a stand near the sofa and began to read. *"A quarter of an hour passed,"* Keckley remembered, *"and on glancing at the sofa the face of the president seemed more cheerful. The dejected look was gone; in fact, the countenance was lighted up with new resolution and hope."* Wanting to see what he was reading, Keckley pretended she had dropped something and went behind where Lincoln was sitting so that she could look over his shoulder. It was the Book of Job.

Lincoln learned to use faith in God's Word to manage his melancholy (depression). *Abraham Lincoln fought clinical depression all his life. His condition was indeed a character issue: it gave him the tools to save the nation.* — Joshua Wolf Shenk

The depression drove Lincoln to God's word and there he received even greater strength beyond his ability to overcome the depression and lead a nation. He struggled with it from time to time, but it did not defeat him, as long as He sought God and His word.

Scriptures on Overcoming Depression

Deuteronomy 31:8 — And the Lord, he it is that doth go before thee; he will be with thee, he will not fail thee, neither forsake thee: fear not, neither be dismayed.

Deuteronomy 33:27 — The eternal God is thy refuge, and underneath are the everlasting arms: and he shall thrust out the enemy from before thee; and shall say, Destroy them.

2 Samuel 22:17-22 — "He reached down from on high and took hold of me; he drew me out of deep waters. [18] He rescued me from my powerful enemy, from my foes, who were too strong for me. [19] They confronted me in the day of my disaster, but the LORD was my support. [20] He brought me out into a spacious place; he rescued me because he delighted in me. [21] "The LORD has dealt with me according to my righteousness; according to the cleanness of my hands he has rewarded me. 22 For I have kept the ways of the LORD; I am not guilty of turning from my God.

2 Samuel 22:29 — For thou art my lamp, O LORD: and the LORD will lighten my darkness.

Psalms 9:9 — The LORD also will be a refuge for the oppressed, a refuge in times of trouble.

Psalm 27:14 — Wait on the LORD: be of good courage, and He shall strengthen thine heart: wait, I say, on the LORD.

Psalms 32:7-9 — Thou art my hiding place; thou shalt preserve me from trouble; thou shalt compass me about with songs of deliverance. Selah. 8 I will instruct thee and teach thee in the way which thou shalt go: I will guide thee with mine eye. 9 Be ye not as the horse, or as the mule, which have no understanding: whose mouth must be held in with bit and bridle, lest they come near unto thee.

Psalm 31:22,24 — For I said in my haste, I am cut off from before thine eyes: nevertheless thou heardest the voice of my supplications when I cried unto thee... 24 Be of good courage, and he shall strengthen your heart, all ye that hope in the Lord.

Psalm 34:18-19 — The Lord is nigh unto them that are of a broken heart; and saveth such as be of a contrite spirit. 19 Many are the afflictions of the righteous: but the Lord delivereth him out of them all.

Psalm 37:23-24 — The steps of a good man are ordered by the Lord: and he delighteth in his way. 24 Though he fall, he shall not be utterly cast down: for the Lord upholdeth him with his hand.

Psalm 42:5 — Why art thou cast down, O my soul? and why art thou disquieted in me? hope thou in God: for I shall yet praise him for the help of his countenance.

Psalm 43:5 — Why art thou cast down, O my soul? and why art thou disquieted within me? hope in God: for I shall yet praise him, who is the health of my countenance, and my God.

Psalm 55:22 — Cast thy burden upon the Lord, and he shall sustain thee: he shall never suffer the righteous to be moved.

Psalm 62:5 — My soul, wait thou only upon God; for my expectation is from him.

Psalm 71:5 — For thou art my hope, O Lord God: thou art my trust from my youth.

Psalm 126:5 — They that sow in tears shall reap in joy.

Psalm 143:7-8 — Hear me speedily, O Lord: my spirit faileth: hide not thy face from me, lest I be like unto them that go down into the pit. [8] Cause me to hear thy lovingkindness in the morning; for in thee do I trust: cause me to know the way wherein I should walk; for I lift up my soul unto thee.

Psalm 147:3 — He healeth the broken in heart, and bindeth up their wounds.

Psalm 145:14 — The Lord upholdeth all that fall, and raiseth up all those that be bowed down.

Proverbs 12:25 — Heaviness in the heart of man maketh it stoop: but a good word maketh it glad.

Proverbs 23:18 — For surely there is an end; and thine expectation shall not be cut off.

Isaiah 26:3-4, Thou wilt keep him in perfect peace, whose mind is stayed on thee: because he trusteth in thee. [4] Trust ye in the Lord for ever: for in the LORD JEHOVAH is everlasting strength: (Perfect means complete. If I keep my part of the promise by staying steadfastly focused on the Lord Jesus Christ, He will keep His promise to give me His perfect peace. See also Philippians 4:6-7 below)

Isaiah 35:10 — And the ransomed of the Lord shall return, and come to Zion with songs and everlasting joy upon their heads: they shall obtain joy and gladness, and sorrow and sighing shall flee away.

Isaiah 40:31, But they that wait upon the Lord shall renew their strength; they shall mount up with wings as eagles; they shall run, and not be weary; and they shall walk, and not faint.

Isaiah 53:4 — Surely he hath borne our griefs, and carried our sorrows: yet we did esteem him stricken, smitten of God, and afflicted.

2 Chronicles 20:17 — Ye shall not need to fight in this battle: set yourselves, stand ye still, and see the salvation of the Lord with you, O Judah and Jerusalem: fear not, nor be dismayed; to morrow go out against them: for the Lord will be with you.

Mark 9:23 — Jesus said unto him, If thou canst believe, all things are possible to him that believeth.

John 14:27 — Peace I leave with you, my peace I give unto you: not as the world giveth, give I unto you. Let not your heart be troubled, neither let it be afraid.

Romans 15:13 — Now the God of hope fill you with all joy and peace in believing, that ye may abound in hope, through the power of the Holy Ghost.

II Corinthians 7:6-7 — Nevertheless God, that comforteth those that are cast down, comforted us by the coming of Titus;

[7] And not by his coming only, but by the consolation wherewith he was comforted in you, when he told us your earnest desire, your mourning, your fervent mind toward me; so that I rejoiced the more.

Philippians 4:6-7 — Be careful for nothing; but in every thing by prayer and supplication with thanksgiving let your requests be made known unto God. [7] And the peace of God, which passeth all understanding, shall keep your hearts and minds through Christ Jesus.

James 4:8 — Draw nigh to God, and he will draw nigh to you. Cleanse your hands, ye sinners; and purify your hearts, ye double minded.

James 4:10 — Humble yourselves in the sight of the Lord, and he shall lift you up.

2 Peter 1:2–3 — Grace and peace be multiplied unto you through the knowledge of God, and of Jesus our Lord, [3] According as his divine power hath given unto us all things that pertain unto life and godliness, through the knowledge of him that hath called us to glory and virtue:

2 Peter 2:9 — The Lord knoweth how to deliver the godly out of temptations...

1 Peter 5:7 — Casting all your care upon him; for he careth for you.

Titus 3:4–7 — But after that the kindness and love of God our Saviour toward man appeared, [5] Not by works of righteousness which we have done, but according to his mercy he saved us, by the washing of regeneration, and renewing of the Holy Ghost; [6] Which he shed on us abundantly through Jesus Christ our Saviour; [7] That being justified by his grace, we should be made heirs according to the hope of eternal life.

2 Peter 1:2–3 — Grace and peace be multiplied unto you through the knowledge of God, and of Jesus our Lord, ³ According as his divine power hath given unto us all things that pertain unto life and godliness, through the knowledge of him that hath called us to glory and virtue:

Conclusion

We may never understand completely why God allows weaknesses in our lives like feelings of depression, suicide, hopelessness and even helplessness. But we do know as many others have found to be true that when we turn to God and His word, He strengthens us in our person, and we experience a new strength we did not have before.

Our hope is restored, those feelings of depression and hopelessness, and weakness are pushed back, and we can go on and do great things in life. As the scriptures state in II Corinthians 12:9; And he said unto me, My grace is sufficient for thee: for my strength is made perfect in weakness. Most gladly therefore will I rather glory in my infirmities, that the power of Christ may rest upon me.

CHAPTER 5

The Futility Of Worry

(LUKE 12:22-34)

Introduction

To worry is to invite fear, anxiety, depression, ulcers and a host of other problems. To have faith is *to defeat fear, anxiety, depression, ulcers and a host of other problems.* The parable we will be studying is advice given by the greatest authority on life, Jesus. It would be to our greatest advantage to listen to His counsel.

Reading of the Parable in Luke 12:22-34

And he said unto his disciples, Therefore I say unto you, Take no thought for your life, what ye shall eat; neither for the body, what ye shall put on. 23 The life is more than meat, and the body is more than raiment. 24 Consider the ravens: for they neither sow nor reap; which neither have storehouse nor barn; and God feedeth them: how much more are ye better than the fowls? 25 And which of you with taking thought can add to his stature one cubit? 26 If ye then be not able to do that thing which is least, why take ye thought for the rest? 27 Consider the lilies how they grow: they toil not, they spin not; and yet I say unto you, that Solomon in all his glory was not arrayed like one of these. 28 If then God so clothe the grass, which is to day in the field, and to morrow is cast into the oven; how much more will he clothe you, O ye of little faith? [29] And seek not ye what ye shall eat, or what ye shall drink, neither be ye of doubtful mind. [30] For all these things do the nations of the world seek after: and your Father knoweth that ye have need of these things. [31] But rather seek ye the kingdom of God; and all these things shall be added unto you. [32] Fear not, little flock; for it is your Father's good pleasure to give you the kingdom. [33] Sell that ye have, and give alms; provide yourselves bags which wax not old, a treasure in the heavens that faileth not, where no thief approacheth, neither moth corrupteth. [34] For where your treasure is, there will your heart be also.

Commentary on Parable

Christ largely insisted upon this caution not to give way to troubling, perplexing cares. The arguments here used are for our encouragement to cast our care upon God, which is the right way to get peace. As in our size, so in our state, it is our wisdom to take life as it is and allow the Lord to make something new and exciting of it.

An eager, anxious pursuit of the things of this world, even necessary things, can bring worry to the disciples of Christ. Fears must not prevail. When we frighten ourselves with thoughts of evil to come, and take on needless cares, we can avoid it all by believing and practicing His words to *fear not*.

If we value the beauty of holiness, we shall not crave the luxuries of life. Let us then examine whether we belong to the family of God. Christ should be our Master, and we are His servants; not only working servants, but waiting servants. We must be men that wait for their Lord, that sit up while he stays out late, to be ready to receive Him. In this Christ alluded to his own ascension to heaven, His coming to call his people to him by death on the cross, and His return to judge the world.

We are uncertain as to the time of his coming to us, we should therefore be always ready. If men thus take care of their houses, let us be wise for our souls. Jesus said, Be ye therefore ready also; as ready as the good man of the house would be, if he knew at what hour the thief would come. There is a Kingdom of the Lord and one day it will reign over all the earth, let's be working and seeking His Kingdom and righteousness.

Key Points to Remember

- A simple trust in a caring Father frees one from a nagging anxiety about the physical necessities of life.

- Worry is useless because life is in God's hands.

- God knows our needs better than we do and makes provision for us.

- When our primary aim is the total Lordship of Jesus then material concerns will not distract us. Like the Apostle Paul who learned to be content with much or with little.

- Provision in life follows those whose priorities are concerned with God's ways, work, will and His rule (kingdom).

- Jesus has promised to never leave us or forsake us.

Conclusion

It is the concerns of life that can either cause us to worry or grow in our faith and trust. Jesus is the Master of life; He was there when life began, and He is with us now. When we live according to His ways, we will experience the abundant life Jesus promised, and we will live a less worry filled life, full of faith and joy.

CHAPTER 6

The God Of Restoration

(PSALM 85:1-13)

Introduction

Restoration is a recurring theme in scripture as those who strayed from the teachings and love of **God** sought to restore their divine relationship with Him. Further occurrences of repairing what had decayed included personal relationships, fortunes, and health. We hear of relationships that have been restored, those who have been sick restored to health, and the backslidden restored to a right relationship with the Lord. Truly God restores and makes all things new.

Definition of Restoration

Restoration — Hebrew word is (ar-oo-kaw) — means healing and restoration. restoring to soundness); wholeness (literally or figuratively) — health, made up, perfected.

Reading of Psalms 85: 1-13 (NKJ)

LORD, You have been favorable to your land; You have brought back the captivity of Jacob. ² You have forgiven the iniquity of Your people; You have covered all their sin. Selah ³You have taken away all Your wrath; You have turned from the fierceness of Your anger. ⁴ Restore us, O God of our salvation, And cause Your anger toward us to cease. ⁵ Will You be angry with us forever? Will You prolong Your anger to all generations?

⁶ Will You not revive us again, That Your people may rejoice in You? ⁷ Show us Your mercy, LORD, And grant us Your salvation. ⁸ I will hear what God the LORD will speak, For He will speak peace to His people and to His saints; But let them not turn back to folly. ⁹ Surely His salvation is near to those who fear Him, That glory may dwell in our land. ¹⁰ Mercy and truth have met together; Righteousness and peace have kissed. ¹¹ Truth shall spring out of the earth, And righteousness shall look down from heaven. ¹² Yes, the LORD will give what is good; And our land will yield its increase. ¹³ Righteousness will go before Him And shall make His footsteps our pathway.

Commentary of Psalms 85:1-13

The sense of present afflictions should not do away the remembrance of former mercies. The favor of God is the fountain of happiness to nations, as well as to persons. When God forgives sin, he covers it; and when he covers the sin of his people, he covers it all. See what the pardon of sin is. In compassion to us, when Christ our Intercessor has stood before thee, thou hast turned away thine anger. When we are reconciled to God, then, and not till then, we may expect the comfort of his being reconciled to us. He shows mercy to those to whom he grants salvation; for salvation is of mere mercy.

The Lord's people may expect sharp and tedious afflictions when they commit sin; but when they return to him with humble prayer, he will make them again to rejoice in him. Sooner or later, God will speak peace to his people. If he does not command outward peace, yet he will suggest inward peace, speaking to their hearts by his Spirit. Peace is spoken only to those who turn from sin. All sin is folly, especially backsliding; it is the greatest folly to return to sin. Surely God's salvation is nigh, whatever our difficulties and distresses are.

Also, his honor is secured, that glory may dwell in our land. And the truth of the promises is shown by the Divine mercy in sending the Redeemer. The Divine justice is now satisfied by the great atonement. Christ, the way, truth, and life, sprang out of the earth when He took our nature upon him, and Divine justice looked upon Him well pleased and satisfied. For His sake all good things, especially His Holy Spirit, are given to those who ask Him. Through Christ, the pardoned sinner becomes fruitful in good works, and by looking to and trusting in the Savior's righteousness, finds his feet set in the way of his steps. Righteousness is a sure guide, both in meeting God, and in following Him

Story of Gods Restoration

Jeff grew up in the church, but during high school his dad died suddenly of a heart attack. This devastating event caused him to doubt God, and he eventually "got converted" to the world. He pursued a career in rock music as a "roadie," working on the stage for famous rock bands. Soon his life began to implode with broken relationships and addiction. Months would go by when his family didn't know where he was. Meanwhile, show after show, Jeff would sit backstage wondering, "Is this really all there is to life?" In 2005, Jeff ended up in prison. A conviction on DUI, an addiction to drugs — his life was headed south. And to make matters worse, Jeff's mom informed him of her cancer. In Jeff's mind, he was at the bottom. What more was there?

As Jeff's aunt continued to pray, Jeff's life began to take an unusual turn. Those little booklets and magazines he had been getting began to pique his interest and make more sense. So, Jeff made a deal with God. He would yield his life to Christ if God would cure his mother. He got down on his knees and surrendered his life to God. Jeff's mother had surgery, and today she has no signs of cancer. Doctors say there is no medical treatment that could explain her total healing. Jeff believes it was a miracle! The drugs are history. And he was baptized in the church. His life has been changed forever! And he credits it all to the power of Jesus Christ and the ministry of Amazing Facts. Now that's revival and restoration.

Conclusion

The purpose of the resurrection of Christ is restoration. The death and resurrection of Jesus was given for us to restore our relationship to God once and for all. To restore our lives to what God intended, and to use our lives to bring restoration to fallen humanity. One day He will restore this world to a new heaven and new earth and all that dwells in it. Truly He is the God of restoration.

Chapter 7

Jesus Our Hope In A Hopeless World

Introduction

As Christians we have a futuristic hope of seeing our Savior Jesus face to face. He is the One who saved us by His grace. We can expect a better day is coming, a new world is coming and heaven will be our eternal home. We have a present hope. We have the promises of God that better days are coming, answered prayers, grace for unanswered prayers, grace and strength from our Lord to meet the challenges of life. In all this, Jesus is our hope in this life, and in the life to come.

Hope Defined

Hope in the noun tense in the Greek is (elpis) — is defined as a favorable and confident expectation. It has to do with the unseen and the future. Hope describes the happy anticipation of good (the most frequent meaning) the ground upon which hope is based which is Christ. Hope in the verb tense in the Greek is (elpizo) — is defined as to trust, to trust in and trust on.

Scriptures on Hope

Romans 8:24-25, For we are saved by hope: but hope that is seen is not hope: for what a man seeth, why doth he yet hope for? 25 But if we hope for that we see not, then do we with patience wait for it.

(Note: *We were saved in this hope and wait with expectancy when we see Him either when He comes back again or after we pass from this life).*

I Peter 1:17-21 And if ye call on the Father, who without respect of persons judgeth according to every man's work, pass the time of your sojourning here in fear: 18 Forasmuch as ye know that ye were not redeemed with corruptible things, as silver and gold, from your vain conversation received by tradition from your fathers; 19 But with the precious blood of Christ, as of a lamb without blemish and without spot: 20 Who verily was foreordained before the foundation of the world, but was manifest in these last times for you, 21 Who by him do believe in God, that raised him up from the dead, and gave him glory; that your faith and hope might be in God.

Note: *We are to live this life according to the hope and salvation we have received from Jesus. Faith and Hope work together.*

1 Timothy 1:1-5, Paul, an apostle of Jesus Christ by the commandment of God our Saviour, and Lord Jesus Christ, which is our hope; 2 Unto Timothy, my own son in the faith: Grace, mercy, and peace, from God our Father and Jesus Christ our Lord. 3 As I besought thee to abide still at Ephesus, when I went into

Macedonia, that thou mightest charge some that they teach no other doctrine, ⁴ Neither give heed to fables and endless genealogies, which minister questions, rather than godly edifying which is in faith: so do. ⁵ Now the end of the commandment is charity out of a pure heart, and of a good conscience, and of faith unfeigned:

Note: *There are various false doctrines, new age teachings, eastern religions, etc. that we need to guard against and keep our faith firm in the hope of Christ, His truths, His life and will.*

II Corinthians 1:3-10, Blessed be God, even the Father of our Lord Jesus Christ, the Father of mercies, and the God of all comfort; ⁴ Who comforteth us in all our tribulation, that we may be able to comfort them which are in any trouble, by the comfort wherewith we ourselves are comforted of God. ⁵ For as the sufferings of Christ abound in us, so our consolation also aboundeth by Christ. ⁶ And whether we be afflicted, it is for your consolation and salvation, which is effectual in the enduring of the same sufferings which we also suffer: or whether we be comforted, it is for your consolation and salvation. ⁷ And our hope of you is stedfast, knowing, that as ye are partakers of the sufferings, so shall ye be also of the consolation. ⁸ For we would not, brethren, have you ignorant of our trouble which came to us in Asia, that we were pressed out of measure, above strength, insomuch that we despaired even of life: ⁹ But we had the sentence of death in ourselves, that we should not trust in ourselves, but in God which raiseth the dead: ¹⁰ Who delivered us from so great a death, and doth deliver: in whom we trust that he will yet deliver us;

Note: *The apostle Paul refers to Jesus Our Hope in this life and the* *life to come who comforts us in suffering as he experienced it firsthand and delivers us from suffering.*

Romans15: 12-13, And again, Esaias saith, There shall be a root of Jesse, and he that shall rise to reign over the Gentiles; in him shall the Gentiles trust. [13] Now the God of hope fill you with all joy and peace in believing, that ye may abound in hope, through the power of the Holy Ghost.

Note: *First, we see a prophecy of Jesus coming to reign and giving hope to not only the Jews but the Gentiles (non Jewish heritage). It is the Lord who by His spirit gives us joy and peace as we abound in hope.*

I Corinthians 15:19-24, If in this life only we have hope in Christ, we are of all men most miserable. [20] But now is Christ risen from the dead, and become the firstfruits of them that slept. [21] For since by man came death, by man came also the resurrection of the dead. [22] For as in Adam all die, even so in Christ shall all be made alive. [23] But every man in his own order: Christ the firstfruits; afterward they that are Christ's at his coming. [24] Then cometh the end, when he shall have delivered up the kingdom to God, even the Father; when he shall have put down all rule and all authority and power.

Story of the power of Hope and Faith in God

Some of you may have seen the movie based on a true story; a film titled **The 33** based on the events of a mining disaster was directed by Patricia Riggen and written by Mikko Alanne and Jose Rivera along with Mike Medavoy. The 2010 Copiapó mining accident, also known then as the "Chilean mining accident", began in the afternoon of Thursday, 5 August 2010 as a significant cave-in at the troubled 121-year-old San José copper–gold mine. The mine is located in the Atacama Desert about 45 kilometers (28 mi) north of the regional capital of Copiapó, in northern Chile.[1] The buried men, who became known as "Los 33" ("The 33"), were trapped 700 meters (2,300 ft.) underground and about 5 kilometers (3 mi) from the mine's entrance via spiraling underground service ramps.

The mixed crew of experienced miners and technical support personnel and with less experience working underground, survived for a record of sixty-nine days deep underground, before their rescue. Previous geological instability at the old mine and a long record of safety violations for the mine's owners had resulted in a series of fines and accidents, including eight deaths, during the dozen years leading up to this accident. As a result of the mine's notorious history, it was originally thought that the workers had probably not survived the collapse or would starve to death before they were found, if ever.

Once the rescuers, and the world, knew that the men were alive, Chile implemented a comprehensive plan to both care for the workers during their entrapment and to rescue the miners from the depths. The plan included the deployment of three large, international drilling rig teams, nearly every Chilean government ministry, the expertise of the NASA space agency and more than a dozen multi-national corporations from nearly every continent.

After 69 days trapped deep underground, all 33 men were brought safely to the surface on 13 October 2010 by a winching operation that lasted nearly 24 hours. After winching the last trapped miner to the surface, the mine rescue paramedics, the best available drawn from multiple national agencies and military services, all still underground, held up a sign for the TV cameras reading "Misión cumplida Chile" (English: ""Mission accomplished Chile"), which was seen by a TV and internet audience estimated at more than 1 billion viewers around the world.

The trapped miners, most of whom were Roman Catholic, asked for religious items, including Bibles, crucifixes, rosaries, and statues of the Virgin Mary and other saints to be sent down to them. After Pope Benedict XVI sent each man a rosary, these were brought to the mine by the Archbishop of Santiago, Cardinal Francisco Javier Errázuriz Ossa in person. After three weeks in the mine, one man who was civilly married to his wife 25 years earlier asked her to enter into a sacramental marriage. The men set up a makeshift chapel in the mine, and Mario Gómez, the eldest miner, spiritually counseled his companions and led daily prayers.

Among the miners, a number attributed religious significance to events. Mario Sepúlveda said, *"I was with God, and with the Devil — and God took me."* Mónica Araya, the wife of the first man rescued, Florencio Ávalos, noted: *"We are really religious, both my husband and I, so God was always present. It is a miracle, this rescue was so difficult, it's a grand miracle."* As one story in the British newspaper Daily Mail reported, "A deep religious faith powered this rescue; miners and families and rescuers alike believe their prayers were answered."

Conclusion

When a man or woman has hope in the Lord anything can be endured and overcome. In Hebrews 6:10-20, For God is not unjust to forget your work and labor of love which you have shown toward His name, in that you have ministered to the saints, and do minister. 11 And we desire that each one of you show the same diligence to the full assurance of hope until the end, 12 that you do not become sluggish, but imitate those who through faith and patience inherit the promises.

God's Infallible Purpose in Christ

For God is not unrighteous to forget your work and labour of love, which ye have shewed toward his name, in that ye have ministered to the saints, and do minister. 11 And we desire that every one of you do shew the same diligence to the full assurance of hope unto the end: 12 That ye be not slothful, but followers of them who through faith and patience inherit the promises. 13 For when God made promise to Abraham, because he could swear by no greater, he sware by himself, 14 Saying, Surely blessing I will bless thee, and multiplying I will multiply thee. 15 And so, after he had patiently endured, he obtained the promise. 16 For men verily swear by the greater: and an oath for confirmation is to them an end of all strife. 17 Wherein God, willing more abundantly to shew unto the heirs of promise the immutability of his counsel, confirmed it by an oath:

18 That by two immutable things, in which it was impossible for God to lie, we might have a strong consolation, who have fled for refuge to lay hold upon the hope set before us: 19 Which hope we have as an anchor of the soul, both sure and stedfast, and which entereth into that within the veil; 20 Whither the forerunner is for

us entered, even Jesus, made an high priest for ever after the order of Melchisedec.

Let us hold fast to Jesus for He is that anchor to our soul that gives us hope in a hopeless world.

CHAPTER 8

I Will Give You Rest

(MATTHEW 11:28-30)

Introduction

There is nothing as refreshing as rest and renewal as we look at the following true story. The IRONMAN TRIATHLON© is one of the most grueling endurance events in the world. To complete the race, an athlete must swim 2.4 miles, ride a bicycle 112 more miles, and then run a 26.2-mile marathon. The best athletes in the world can complete this monumental challenge in under nine hours. But for Australian Chris Legh, his Ironman experience in 1997 was memorable for the wrong reasons.

Known as one of the top competitors in the sport, he was unable to keep any fluids or food down during the race. As a result, he became dehydrated, leading to several of his organs shutting down. Fifty yards from the finish line, his body completely gave out. Legh never finished the race and would've died without immediate medical attention. Thankfully, he recovered and has won two Ironman events since. But first, he had to be restored.

While experiences like Legh's show us humans have physical limits to their endurance, the same can also be said about their spiritual lives. Thankfully, there are warning signs that exist before it becomes too late. When people don't want to read their Bible or pray, if they decide to shut people out of their lives, or if church becomes just a ritual, something deeper may be going on. They may be suffering from spiritual dehydration.

Just as a "Low Fuel" light tells us to fill up the car with gas, it's time to ask God for a renewed spirit when we see these warning signs. Consider that Jesus had crowds following him everywhere, but he knew his spiritual limits so well that he consistently took time to recharge, even when death was near (see Luke 22:39-43).

When your life's "Low Fuel" light comes on, don't ignore it. God wants to recharge and renew your life. Allow him to do just that. Make sure you accept His help to cross the finish line of life. In this chapter we will be looking at the promises of Jesus to give us rest. Nothing can compare to the rest Jesus promised us as we come to Him and receive rest and renewal to our very soul and spirit.

Thoughts and Definitions of Rest

Rest is one of the greatest gifts God gave to mankind. Rest is synonymous to peace. Naturally, we associate rest with sleep. When we are tired, we think of sleeping and resting. After that, we are refreshed and energized to move out again. We feel good and happy. This is not God's rest I want to talk about here. You ask what is God's rest? God 's rest is deep and profound. It supersedes the rest derived when we are physically tired or sleepy or worn out from each day's labor; It is a rest that heals and makes you whole. Rest and peace are synonymous. It is a rest that calms your fears and gives you a sense of stability to face the future with confidence, regardless of what is happening around you.

It is a kind of peace that allows you to always be in a state of rest — in trials and joyful times, because you are trusting the Lord. "Thou wilt keep him in perfect peace, whose mind is stayed on thee: because he trusted on thee. Trust ye in the Lord forever, for in the Lord JEHOVAH is everlasting strength." Isaiah 26:3-4.

The Hebrew word for rest is nuach- it means to rest, to be quiet. Sometimes, it is synonymous to shabat- to cease or to rest.

The Greek word for rest in this key verse is anapausis meaning cessation, refreshment. Christ's rest is not a rest from work, but in work, not the rest of activity, but of the harmonious working of all the faculties and affections, of will, heart, imagination, conscience- because each has found in God the ideal sphere of its satisfaction and development. In other words, the peace of God through the Holy Spirit has come to indwell the hearts of men and women who trust Him fully.

Reading of Matthew 11:28-30

28 Come unto me, all ye that labour and are heavy laden, and I will give you rest. 29 Take my yoke upon you, and learn of me; for I am meek and lowly in heart: and ye shall find rest unto your souls. 30 For my yoke is easy, and my burden is light.

Consider the following:

- We must first humble ourselves and come to Jesus.

- All of us from time to time become weary and heavy laden. To be weary is to be exhausted and to be heavy laden is to be overburdened with the cares and concerns of this life. It would be like weighing down an animal with heavy loads.

- Jesus promises that if we come to Him with all our burdens, He will give us rest. The Greek word (anapausis) means refreshment. It is not a rest from work but in work, not the rest of inactivity but of the harmonious working of all the faculties and affections, of will, heart and mind, conscience. The reason is because each has found in God the ideal sphere for its satisfaction and development. It is peace like a river down in our souls.

- Jesus tells us to take His yoke, the Greek word (zugos) means serving two things together. Concerning submission to authority, so Christ's yoke is not simply imparted by Him but shared with Him.

- Jesus invites us to learn from Him, for He is gentle and humble in heart. When we are yoked with Him, His character will have an influence on our lives, and we also will develop a gentleness and humility in our lives. There is a humbleness of heart that is genuine, not an outward pretending to be humble.

The Greek word for gentleness is epieeikes means moderate, mild, fair, forbearing.it doesn't insist on the letter of the law but expresses that considerateness that looks humanely and reasonably at the facts of a case. (Example: Rebellious students at a bible college and how a teacher Brother Gatchel handled the situation by asking the staff to give them another chance. He gave these students the opportunity to make things right by apologizing to the whole student body for their inappropriate actions).

- We will find rest for our souls. Jesus is speaking about a deep renewing rest that touches the very depths of our being as it affects our living.

- For His Yoke is easy and His burden is light. The yoke is easy, and the burden is light because He carries the greater weight. As we are yoked with His strength, and we allow Him to carry our burdens we will experience the abundant life Jesus spoke about.

Commentary on this Verse: 25-30

It's becoming of children, to be grateful. When we come to God as a Father, we must remember that He is Lord of heaven and earth, which obliges us to come to him with reverence as to the sovereign Lord of all; yet with confidence, as one able to defend us from evil, and to supply us with all good. Our blessed Lord added a remarkable declaration, that the Father had delivered into his hands all power, authority, and judgment. We are indebted to Christ for all the revelation we have of God the Father's will and love, ever since Adam sinned.

Our Saviour has invited all that labour and are heavy-laden, to come unto him. In some senses all men are so. Worldly men burden themselves with fruitless cares for wealth and honours; the careless and the sensual labour in pursuit of pleasures; the slave of Satan and his own lusts, is the merest drudge on earth. Those who labour to establish their own righteousness also labour in vain. The convinced sinner is heavy-laden with guilt and terror; and the tempted and afflicted believer has labours and burdens.

Christ invites all to come to Him to rest their souls. He alone gives this invitation; men come to him, when, feeling their guilt and misery, and believing his love and power to help, they seek him in fervent prayer. Thus, it is the duty and interest of weary and heavy-laden sinners, to come to Jesus Christ. This is the gospel call; Whoever will, let him come. All who thus come will receive rest as Christ's gift and obtain peace and comfort in their hearts. But in coming to him they must take his yoke and submit to his authority.

They must learn of Him all things, as to their comfort and obedience. He accepts the willing servant, however imperfect the services. Here we may find rest for our souls, and here only. Nor need we fear his yoke. His commandments are holy, just, and good. It requires self-denial, and exposes to difficulties, but this is abundantly repaid, even in this world, by inward peace and joy. It is a yoke that is lined with love. So powerful is the assistance He gives us, so suitable the encouragement, and so strong the consolations to be found in the way of duty, that we may truly say, it is a yoke of pleasantness and of blessing.

The way of duty is the way of rest. The truths Christ teaches are such as we may venture our souls upon. Such is the Redeemer's mercy; and why should the labouring and burdened sinner seek for rest from any other source? But forced obedience, far from being easy and light, is a heavy burden. In vain do we draw near to Jesus with our lips, while the heart is far from him. Then come to Jesus to find true rest for your souls.

Conclusion

Let us come to Him daily, for deliverance, from wrath and guilt, from sin and Satan, from all our cares, fears, and sorrows. We need to stay closely yoked to our Lord. For truly, He alone gives the true rest and salvation, this world desperately needs.

CHAPTER 9

Importance Of Not Losing Our Joy

(JOHN 8:31-36)

Introduction

Have you lost your joy in the Lord? The word of God states that the joy of the Lord is our strength. Joy is vital and is a very important part of our spiritual life. We will be exploring the scriptures on the importance of keeping joy in our walk with Christ.

Definition of Joy

The Greek word for joy as a noun is (Chara) means *delight* similar to Greek verb (chairo) to rejoice found often in the Gospels and shown as gladness. It is a fruit of the spirit marked by the grace of God where there is an inward sense of joy regardless of circumstances, a sense of rejoicing even in the midst of sorrow.

Scriptures on Joy
Joy is not dependent upon our circumstance

Psalm 27:5-7, For in the time of trouble he shall hide me in his pavilion: in the secret of his tabernacle shall he hide me; he shall set me up upon a rock. ⁶ And now shall mine head be lifted up above mine enemies round about me: therefore will I offer in his tabernacle sacrifices of joy; I will sing, yea, I will sing praises unto the LORD. ⁷ Hear, O LORD, when I cry with my voice: have mercy also upon me, and answer me.

We can be in a difficult situation and yet experience joy.

Jesus added to this by saying, "Blessed are ye, when men shall hate you, and when they shall separate you from their company, and shall reproach you, and cast out your name as evil, for the Son of man's sake. ²³ Rejoice ye in that day, and leap for joy: for, behold, your reward is great in heaven: for in the like manner did their fathers unto the prophets." — **Luke 6:22-23**

Though joy cannot be forced, it can be experienced in difficult situations.

James adds to this thought with, "My brethren, count it all joy when ye fall into divers temptations; ³ Knowing this, that the trying of your faith worketh patience." — **James 1:2-3.**

Joy is possible when we feel secure in the Lord.

Psalm 4:6-8 Many, Lord, are asking, "There be many that say, Who will shew us any good? LORD, lift thou up the light of thy countenance upon us. ⁷ Thou hast put gladness in my heart, more than in the time that their corn and their wine increased. ⁸ I will both lay me down in peace, and sleep: for thou, LORD, only makest me dwell in safety."

While others link their happiness to prosperity, believers can find joy in the Lord. When we add our voice to David's and proclaim, "You alone, Lord," will be the lifter of my head. In you alone will I place my trust. Whether I am rich or poor, have an active career, or I can't find a job, I am safe with you.

Paul wrote, "Rejoice in the Lord always: and again I say, Rejoice. ⁵ Let your moderation be known unto all men. The Lord is at hand." **Philippians 4:4-5**

Joy comes when we have a clear direction for our life.

We might also use the word purpose. The following verses about joy illustrate this principle: **Psalm 16:11(NIV),** You make known to me the path of life; you will fill me with joy in your presence, with eternal pleasures at your right hand.

Jesus said, "The kingdom of heaven is like treasure hidden in a field. When a man found it, he hid it again, and then in his joy went and sold all he had and bought that field" — **Matthew 13:44 (NIV).**

Where is your hidden treasure? What is the path of life that God has for you? Are you seeking the fields for the treasure that God has for you? Is Jesus that treasure in your heart and life?

Joy comes when we live in God's presence

Psalm 21:5-7 (NIV). Through the victories you gave, his glory is great; you have bestowed on him splendor and majesty. Surely you have granted him unending blessings and made him glad about the joy of your presence. For the king trusts in the Lord; through the unfailing love of the Most High he will not be shaken.

In a world where celebrity, success, and money are glorified, it is easy to lose focus on what brings real joy. Put simply, this verse says, victories are good, glory is great, and splendor and majesty are their results, but my joy comes when I spend time in God's presence.

Joy comes when we spend our life Praising God

Psalm 27:6 And now shall mine head be lifted up above mine enemies round about me: therefore will I offer in his tabernacle sacrifices of joy; I will sing, yea, I will sing praises unto the LORD.

Psalm 47:1-3 O clap your hands, all ye people; shout unto God with the voice of triumph. ² For the LORD most high is terrible; he is a great King over all the earth. ³ He shall subdue the people under us, and the nations under our feet.

Psalm 71:23 My lips shall greatly rejoice when I sing unto thee; and my soul, which thou hast redeemed.

Singing, clapping, and shouting are all a part of joyful worship. These three scriptures about joy only scratch the surface of examples of praise. Here is another example of praise found in Luke, "As he went along, people spread their cloaks on the road. When he came near the place where the road goes down the Mount of Olives, the whole crowd of disciples began joyfully to praise God in loud voices for all the miracles they had seen.

Joy comes when we live an honest Biblical life

Psalm 97:10-12 Ye that love the LORD, hate evil: he preserveth the souls of his saints; he delivereth them out of the hand of the wicked. [11] Light is sown for the righteous, and gladness for the upright in heart. [12] Rejoice in the LORD, ye righteous; and give thanks at the remembrance of his holiness.

Perhaps the idea of honesty doesn't seem to fit with principles of joy, but let's look at the opposite side briefly. Dishonesty leads to guilt, and discouragement, while honesty breeds satisfaction, and peace. When we add the concept of Biblical honesty, then we discover true joy.

Jesus offers His truth on being obedient to His word. He says in **John 15:10-12, (NIV)** "If you keep my commands, you will remain in my love, just as I have kept my Father's commands and remain in his love. I have told you this so that my joy may be in you and that your joy may be full and complete. My command is this: Love each other as I have loved you."

There is no greater place to live than in the center of God's will. There is no way to be in the center of his will without living according to the word of God. An honest Biblical based life leads to a joyful life.

Joy comes when people see Christ in us, and exclude us from their ungodly gatherings

Psalm 119:23-24 Princes also did sit and speak against me: but thy servant did meditate in thy statutes. [24] Thy testimonies also are my delight and my counselors.

Quite often we feel bad when we are left out of activities, thinking that there is something wrong with us. But is it possible that they leave us out because there is something right about us? David spoke of those with evil motives.

Even when David's enemies were hunting him down and closing in, he was able to compose joyful psalms of praise to God. He rejoiced in his understanding that God, His Father, could flatten any army, resolve any conflict, and confuse the plans of those who sought to kill him. He was joyful in the Lord. — Ronald f. Youngblood, Nelson's New Illustrated Bible Dictionary.

A similar situation of opposition occurred in the book of Acts:

"And the word of the Lord was published throughout all the region. 50 But the Jews stirred up the devout and honourable women, and the chief men of the city, and raised persecution against Paul and Barnabas, and expelled them out of their coasts. 51 But they shook off the dust of their feet against them, and came unto Iconium. 52 And the disciples were filled with joy, and with the Holy Ghost." — **Acts 13:49-52.**

There are several other instances where Paul encouraged people who were insulted or rejected because of their faith. He always encouraged them to be joyful because they were suffering on behalf of Christ.

When people don't want you around because of your faith, celebrate joyfully. You are being excluded because they see Jesus living in you.

Personal Experience

I remember when I worked for the City someone showed me a list of invited guests to a manager's party. At the end of the List were these words *"Not To Be Invited"* under it was my name and 2 other people who were Christians.

Conclusion

The next time you are mocked, left out, ignored or treated unfairly remember this truth and rejoice, found in **I Peter 4:14** — If ye be reproached for the name of Christ, happy are ye; for the spirit of glory and of God resteth upon you: on their part he is evil spoken of, but on your part he is glorified.

For this day is holy unto our Lord: neither be ye sorry; for the joy of the Lord is your strength. (Nehemiah 8:10b).

CHAPTER 10

In Our Weakness He Made Us Strong

(II CORINTHIANS 12:9-10)

Introduction

We all admire strength and self-confidence. People who are self-assured and assertive usually move ahead in life. What about those who are weak in certain areas of their life, can they too move ahead and succeed in life. Unless that person knows Jesus he will have a difficult time moving ahead and succeeding in life and will meet with failure more often. The Greek word for weakness is astheneia —want or lack of strength, weakness, illness, suffering, calamity, frailty. Yet the bible promises that in our weakness He is made strong, and His power is perfected in our weaknesses. Let's look at scripture and see how this can be possible through Christ.

Key Scripture II Corinthians 12:6-10

For though I would desire to glory, I shall not be a fool; for I will say the truth: but now I forbear, lest any man should think of me above that which he seeth me to be, or that he heareth of me. ⁷ And lest I should be exalted above measure through the abundance of the revelations, there was given to me a thorn in the flesh, the messenger of Satan to buffet me, lest I should be exalted above measure. [8] For this thing I besought the Lord thrice, that it might depart from me. [9] And he said unto me, My grace is sufficient for thee: for my strength is made perfect in weakness. Most gladly therefore will I rather glory in my infirmities, that the power of Christ may rest upon me. [10] Therefore I take pleasure in infirmities, in reproaches, in necessities, in persecutions, in distresses for Christ's sake: for when I am weak, then am I strong.

Commentary from Matthew Henry

"The apostle gives an account of the method God took to keep him humble, and to prevent his being lifted up above measure, on account of the visions and revelations he had. We are not told what this thorn in the flesh was, whether some great trouble, or some great temptation. But God often brings this good out of evil, that the reproaches of our enemies help to hide pride from us. If God loves us, he will keep us from being exalted above measure; and spiritual burdens are ordered to cure spiritual pride.

This thorn in the flesh is said to be a messenger of Satan which he sent for evil; but God designed it, and overruled it for good. Prayer is a salve for every sore, a remedy for every malady; and when we are afflicted with thorns in the flesh, we should give ourselves to prayer. If an answer be not given to the first prayer, nor to the second, we are to continue praying. Troubles are sent to teach us to pray; and are continued, to teach us to continue instant in prayer.

Though God accepts the prayer of faith, yet he does not always give what is asked for: as he sometimes grants in wrath, so he sometimes denies in love. When God does not take away our troubles and temptations, yet, if he gives grace enough for us, we have no reason to complain. Grace signifies the good-will of God towards us, and that is enough to enlighten and enliven us, sufficient to strengthen and comfort in all afflictions and distresses. His strength is made perfect in our weakness. Thus his grace is manifested and magnified. When we are weak in ourselves, then we are strong in the grace of our Lord Jesus Christ; when we feel that we are weak in ourselves, then we go to Christ, receive strength from him, and enjoy most of the supplies of Divine strength and grace".

Practical Aspects of Weakness

1. Weakness keeps us humble and keeps us from being proud.

2. God does allow even satan to buffet us to keep us dependent on the Lord.

3. God uses weakness to show His power and glory.

4. God's strength is made perfect in our weakness. It causes us to be dependent on the Lord's grace.

5. When we are weak in an area of our lives it makes us more open to receive God's power. This is brought to our attention through the life of the apostle Paul. We can note that his experience albeit hard to deal with at times, still the Lord received the glory in it.

Scriptures on Weakness

Matthew 26:41-Watch and pray, that ye enter not into

temptation: the spirit indeed is willing, but the flesh is weak.

1 Corinthians 1:27-29 — But God hath chosen the foolish things of the world to confound the wise; and God hath chosen the weak things of the world to confound the things which are mighty; [28] And base things of the world, and things which are despised, hath God chosen, yea, and things which are not, to bring to nought things that are: [29] That no flesh should glory in his presence.

1 Corinthians 2:2-5 — For I determined not to know any thing among you, save Jesus Christ, and him crucified. [3] And I was with you in weakness, and in fear, and in much trembling. [4] And my speech and my preaching was not with enticing words of man's wisdom, but in demonstration of the Spirit and of power: [5] That your faith should not stand in the wisdom of men, but in the power of God.

Isaiah 40:29-31- He giveth power to the faint; and to them that have no might he increaseth strength. [30] Even the youths shall faint and be weary, and the young men shall utterly fall: [31] But they that wait upon the LORD shall renew their strength; they shall mount up with wings as eagles; they shall run, and not be weary; and they shall walk, and not faint.

Jeremiah 31:25 — "For I have satiated the weary soul, and I have replenished every sorrowful soul."

Romans 8:26 — Likewise the Spirit also helpeth our infirmities: for we know not what we should pray for as we ought: but the Spirit itself maketh intercession for us with groanings which cannot be uttered.

Ezekiel 34:16 — I will seek that which was lost, and bring again that which was driven away, and will bind up that which was broken, and will strengthen that which was sick: but I will destroy the fat and the strong; I will feed them with judgment.

Hebrews 11:33, 34 — Who through faith subdued kingdoms, wrought righteousness, obtained promises, stopped the mouths of lions. [34] Quenched the violence of fire, escaped the edge of the sword, out of weakness were made strong, waxed valiant in fight, turned to flight the armies of the aliens.

Romans 14:1 — Him that is weak in the faith receive ye, but not to doubtful disputations.

1 Corinthians 9:22 — To the weak became I as weak, that I might gain the weak: I am made all things to all men, that I might by all means save some.

Matthew 8:26 — And he saith unto them, Why are ye fearful, O ye of little faith? Then he arose, and rebuked the winds and the sea; and there was a great calm.

Matthew 14:30-31 — But when he saw the wind boisterous, he was afraid; and beginning to sink, he cried, saying, Lord, save me. [31] And immediately Jesus stretched forth his hand, and caught him, and said unto him, O thou of little faith, wherefore didst thou doubt?

Story of a Great Weakness, A Pastors confession
By Pastor Rick Warren of Saddleback Church

Saddleback Church is an evangelical Christian megachurch located in Lake Forest, California, situated in southern Orange County, affiliated with the Southern Baptist Convention. The church was founded in 1980 by Pastor Rick Warren. Weekly church attendance averages over 20,000 people, currently making it the seventh-largest church in the United States (this ranking includes multi-site churches). Saddleback Church currently has 9 regional campuses (not including the Lake Forest campus): San Clemente, Irvine South, Irvine North, Corona, Huntington Beach, San Juan Capistrano, Anaheim (The Grove), Laguna Woods, Los Angeles and 4 international campuses: South Manila, Philippines, Hong Kong, Buenos Aires, Argentina and Berlin, Germany. Several more campuses are planned in the next few years. In addition, Saddleback is "virtually" attended online by those around the country and the world who watch and listen to worship services on demand.

Pastor Warren states that *"instead of hiding and denying our weaknesses, we need to learn to recognize them. We need to learn to share them. And we need to learn to glory in our weaknesses.*

"If God is ever going to use you greatly, you'll walk with a limp the rest of your life. I have struggled with a handicap all my life. I was born with a brain disorder. My staff knows about it. My church knows about it. My prayer team knows about it. I was born with a disorder in my brain chemistry that makes public speaking excruciatingly painful for me. It is a genetic problem that is resistant to any medication.

In a nutshell, my brain overreacts to adrenaline. I'm allergic to adrenaline. First, I get very dizzy. My vision blurs and then it blacks out. Sometimes I get headaches — severe headaches and sometimes severe hot flashes. Any of you who have ever seen me speak have seen me wipe my face. But the most common reaction to this is an absolute sense of irrational panic. Sometimes I'm speaking and I cannot even see the audience.

One of the things I've figured out is that God has used this to build a praying church at Saddleback. I wouldn't think of preaching without having my prayer team praying for me during the message. And they pray for me during each service through the entire service. What's the lesson? God uses weak people! Paul had a handicap, and he said, "I glory in my weakness." It is an absolute myth that you must be a superhuman being to be effective in ministry. The goal is to last. What kind of ministries last? Ones that are real and authentic and vulnerable and honest and non-hypocritical about our weaknesses."

Conclusion

We all have weaknesses as well as strengths in our lives. It is during those times of weakness that we are not to turn to the world and its ways of dealing with weakness, but to the Lord. When we turn to Him and cry out for His help it shows our dependence on Him. We learn to trust His word which holds His promises.

We will then experience the supernatural power of the Lord. For the Lord is a God of power and might who is able to deliver and strengthen us for the battles of life that we all will encounter in this life. Let us remember the words of the Lord to the apostle Paul in **II Corinthians 12:9** — And he said unto me, My grace is sufficient for thee: for my strength is made perfect in weakness. Most gladly therefore will I rather glory in my infirmities, that the power of Christ may rest upon me.

Chapter 11

Jesus Our Crisis Manager

(John 2:5)

Introduction

We all love heroes. We're on the edge of our seats, especially when they are in a crisis. We see that the odds are against them and there appears to be no way out. What we admire is that they keep their fear under control, show courage, and self-control. They use their head, and then the solution comes to them. They do something that completely throws off their opponent and they win over the crisis.

Definition and Examples of Crisis Situations

A. Crisis defined

Greek word (Krisis) — to separate, cut, to cut. A turning point in the course of anything, a decisive or crucial time. A time of great danger or trouble, whose outcome decides whether bad consequences will follow.

B. Examples of Crisis Situations

We live in a world filled with change and crisis. Some of which are wars, terrorist threats, natural disasters, death, human suffering and abductions, all can be seen on the news 24/7. How do these events impact people? What effects have you experienced when you've watched images of the Twin Towers go up in flames, US troops engaged in battle in Iraq, suicide bombings in London, international terrorist attacks, Hurricane Katrina, and national security warnings flash across the TV screen?

Maybe these world crises bring back memories of a personal trauma. The loss of a loved one. The suffering of an automobile accident. A time when you were assaulted. A time when you were abandoned.

Shaky marriages, divorce, death, illness, accidents, terrorist threats, and war arouse in us a crisis response. What happens when crisis or trauma impacts people's lives? How can we prepare and respond to crises as Christians?

Example of How Jesus Handled Crisis at the Wedding in Cana of Galilee

John 2:1-11 And the third day there was a marriage in Cana of Galilee; and the mother of Jesus was there: ² And both Jesus was called, and his disciples, to the marriage. ³ And when they wanted wine, the mother of Jesus saith unto him, They have no wine. ⁴ Jesus saith unto her, Woman, what have I to do with thee? mine hour is not yet come. ⁵ His mother saith unto the servants, Whatsoever he saith unto you, do it. ⁶ And there were set there six waterpots of stone, after the manner of the purifying of the Jews, containing two or three firkins apiece. [7] Jesus saith unto them, Fill the waterpots with water. And they filled them up to the brim. [8] And he saith unto them, Draw out now, and bear unto the governor of the feast. And they bare it. [9] When the ruler of the feast had tasted the water that was made wine, and knew not whence it was: (but the servants which drew the water knew;) the governor of the feast called the bridegroom, [10] And saith unto him, Every man at the beginning doth set forth good wine; and when men have well drunk, then that which is worse: but thou hast kept the good wine until now. [11] This beginning of miracles did Jesus in Cana of Galilee, and manifested forth his glory; and his disciples believed on him.

Commentary on Jesus Turning Water Wine
by James Merritt

"There was not a bigger social event in Jewish life than a wedding. It usually began with a ceremony at sundown in the synagogue. The entire wedding party would leave the synagogue and begin a long candlelight procession through the middle of town. They would pass as many homes as possible so everyone could come out and congratulate them. The couple did not go on a honeymoon; the honeymoon was brought to them. They went home to a party lasting several days. Hospitality at a wedding was considered such a sacred duty that the master of the wedding could be sued for "breach of hospitality." So, running out of food or wine was considered a tremendous insult.

The stone water pots were, as John explained for the benefit of his Gentile readers, used for the Jewish custom of purification. Ceremonial washings were an integral part of first-century Judaism:

The Pharisees and all the Jews do not eat unless they carefully wash their hands, thus observing the traditions of the elders; and when they come from the marketplace, they do not eat unless they cleanse themselves; and there are many other things which they have received in order to observe, such as the washing of cups and pitchers and copper pots. **(Mark 7:3–4)**

The Jews used stone water pots to hold the water used for ritual purification because they believed that, unlike earthenware pots **(Lev. 11:33),** *they did not become unclean. Unlike the smaller one used by the Samaritan woman to draw water from a well. These were large pots, containing twenty or thirty gallons each. Such a large amount of water was needed not only to accommodate the guests, but also because the cooking and eating utensils had to be washed* **(Mark 7:4).**

Mary's faith and confidence in her Son was steadfast. As she had foreseen, He responded by commanding the servants, "Fill the water pots with water." In response, they filled them up to the brim, either by topping them off, or by emptying and refilling them. This seemingly insignificant detail, that the water was up to the very top, shows that nothing was added to the water, and that what followed was indeed a transformation miracle. He ordered the jars to be completely filled before He transformed the water in them into wine, Jesus also showed His miraculous power of provision. Such a large amount of wine (120 to 180 gallons) was more than enough to last for the rest of the celebration.

Jesus came to the rescue of the bride and groom and the celebration continued with the best wine. After the pots were filled,

Jesus instructed the servants to draw some out and take it to the headwaiter. Jewish sources do not make clear whether this individual was the head servant, or a guest chosen to preside over the banquet. In either case, he served as the master of ceremonies at the feast. Since he was responsible for making sure that the guests were supplied with food and drink, the servants took the wine to him.

The headwaiter sampled the food and drink to make sure it was acceptable before it was served to the guests. Therefore, after the servants brought it to him, he tasted the water which had become wine. Though he did not know where it came from (though of course the servants who had drawn the water did), he was astonished at the high quality of this new batch of wine. He called the bridegroom, and said to him, "Every man serves the good wine first, and when the people have drunk freely, and then he serves the poorer wine."

In any case, it was only customary to serve the good wine first and save the poorer wine for later when the people had drunk freely. The verb methusko (drunk freely) literally means "to become drunk," and is so translated in its only other appearances in the New Testament (Luke 12:45; Eph. 5:18). This doesn't mean, this banquet had become a drunken orgy with everyone out of control. The headwaiter was speaking from his own experience. But much to his surprise (and no doubt the groom's as well), it seemed that the groom had kept the good wine until the last. Surely it was the sweetest, freshest, most delightful wine ever tasted. This wine did not come from the normal process of fermentation but was created from nothing. It was created by Jesus, who created all things.

Practical Applications on Handling Crisis situations

- Do what he tells you to do. His mother told the disciples this.
- Jesus will tell us to do our part, no matter how insignificant and we should do it in obedience. For example, He told the disciples to fill the water pots.
- Jesus the Lord of creation does the miracle and turns ordinary water into wine, the best wine they ever drank.
- So, we turn to Jesus when we face problems.
- Talk to Jesus about your problems.
- Obey what he tells you to do.
- Trust Jesus to handle your crisis and He will do the miraculous as you do the practical

Conclusion

In the above story Mary called on Jesus because she knew what matters to us, matters to Jesus. We believe Jesus cares about the big crisis of life such as cancer, loss of a job, divorce, rebellious son or daughter and death. But Jesus also cares about our pets, difficult bosses, flat tires, broken dishes, headaches and heartaches. Jesus never encountered a crisis that He could not handle.

If only the person in crisis would do what He tells them to do, would Jesus come through and provide the miracle needed in that hour. We often assume that obedience follows blessing. In other words when He blesses us first, then our desire to obey Him is intensified. Yet there are those times where Jesus commands us to obey first then blessing will come. Jesus said in John 13:17, "If ye know these things, happy are ye if ye do them."

CHAPTER 12

Lessons From The Book Of Job

Introduction

Job's patience stands out because Job's story is extreme in the amount of suffering he endured. Job lost all his children and his wealth in a single day. He then was covered in painful sores, and his wife offered him no support — she encouraged him to give up, curse God, and die (Job 2:9). When Job's three friends came to comfort him, they could not even recognize him from a distance (Job 2:12). Adding to Job's pain, his friends falsely accused him of wrongdoing and blamed his troubles on his unrepentant heart. Through it all, Job patiently endured (Job 2:10). At the end we see because Job patiently endured the trials and kept his integrity, prayed for his friends and God restored Job. He blessed him with even more than he had before.

Subtopics and scriptures referenced from the New Spirit-Filled Life Bible — noted SFLB

Reading of Scripture in Job 1:1-22

JOB AND HIS FAMILY IN UZ *(SFLB)*
There was a man in the land of Uz, whose name was Job; and

that man was blameless and upright, and one who feared God and shunned evil. ² And seven sons and three daughters were born to him. ³ Also, his possessions were seven thousand sheep, three thousand camels, five hundred yoke of oxen, five hundred female donkeys, and a very large household, so that this man was the greatest of all the people of the East.

⁴ And his sons would go and feast in their houses, each on his appointed day, and would send and invite their three sisters to eat and drink with them. ⁵ So it was, when the days of feasting had run their course, that Job would send and sanctify them, and he would rise early in the morning and offer burnt offerings according to the number of them all. For Job said, "It may be that my sons have sinned and cursed God in their hearts." Thus, Job did regularly.

Satan Attacks Job's Character *(SFLB)*

Now there was a day when the sons of God came to present themselves before the Lord, and Satan also came among them. ⁷ And the Lord said to Satan, "From where do you come?" So, Satan answered the Lord and said, "From going to and fro on the earth, and from walking back and forth on it." ⁸ Then the Lord said to Satan, "Have you considered My servant Job, that there is none like him on the earth, a blameless and upright man, one who fears God and shuns evil?"

⁹ So, Satan answered the Lord and said, "Does Job fear God for nothing? ¹⁰ Have You not made a hedge around him, around his household, and around all that he has on every side? You have blessed the work of his hands, and his possessions have increased in

the land. ¹¹ But now, stretch out Your hand and touch all that he has, and he will surely curse You to Your face!"

¹² And the Lord said to Satan, "Behold, all that he has is in your power; only do not lay a hand on his person." So, Satan went out from the presence of the Lord.

Job Loses His Property and Children *(SFLB)*

¹³ Now there was a day when his sons and daughters were eating and drinking wine in their oldest brother's house; ¹⁴ and a messenger came to Job and said, "The oxen were plowing and the donkeys feeding beside them, ¹⁵ when the Sabeans raided them and took them away — indeed they have killed the servants with the edge of the sword; and I alone have escaped to tell you!"

¹⁶ While he was still speaking, another also came and said, "The fire of God fell from heaven and burned up the sheep and the servants and consumed them; and I alone have escaped to tell you!"

¹⁷ While he was still speaking, another also came and said, "The Chaldeans formed three bands, raided the camels and took them away, yes, and killed the servants with the edge of the sword; and I alone have escaped to tell you!" ¹⁸ While he was still speaking, another also came and said, "Your sons and daughters were eating and drinking wine in their oldest brother's house, ¹⁹ and suddenly a great wind came from across the wilderness and struck the four corners of the house, and it fell on the young people, and they are dead; and I alone have escaped to tell you!"

²⁰ Then Job arose, tore his robe, and shaved his head; and he fell to the ground and worshiped. ²¹ And he said: "Naked I came from my mother's womb, And naked shall I return there. The Lord gave,

and the Lord has taken away; Blessed be the name of the Lord." [22] In all this Job did not sin nor charge God with wrong.

SEVEN LESSONS LEARNED FROM THE BOOK OF JOB

Lesson 1 – God Knows

One of the most overwhelming things about a severe trial can be the sense of isolation. We want to make sure that God knows because when He finds out, surely, He'll do something about it! In the first chapter of Job we are given a behind-the-scenes look at events of which Job was completely unaware. God, however, was very much aware of Job and of the wholehearted obedience he sought to render. In fact, God Himself called Satan's attention to Job. Christ reminded His disciples in **Luke 12:6–7** that God, who even takes detailed note of the sparrows, is much more deeply interested in the affairs of His own children. The Father is aware of everything about us down to the smallest detail. Even the hairs on our heads are numbered.

When we are struck with personal tragedy or persecuted for obedience, we can be sure that God knows. This is vitally important to keep in mind to counteract the sense of isolation and loneliness that will often beset us at such times. "No one understands what I'm going through," we think. But Jesus Christ does! We have a faithful High Priest who was tested in all ways like us and is therefore able to empathize and give us the needed help (**Hebrews 4:15–16**).

Though Job could not begin to understand why all these things were happening to him, he knew God was aware of it. He did not react, as Satan had predicted, by cursing God. Rather, Job told his wife, "Shall we indeed accept good from God, and shall we not accept adversity?" **(Job 2:10).**

Lesson 2 — God Limits the Trial

The story recounted in chapters 1 and 2 makes us privileged to actual conversations between God and Satan! When we begin reading the book of Job, we learn that, while God allowed Satan to afflict Job, He set limits beyond which the devil could not pass. From the start we know there are limits to Job's trial, and we know what those limits are. Initially, God restricted Satan from harming Job's health. Later, He allowed Job to be personally stricken but insisted that his life be spared. In all of this we have an advantage over Job. At the time he was going through adversity, Job knew nothing of the conversation between God and Satan. He knew nothing of any limits God had pre-imposed upon his trial.

When we find ourselves amid great adversity, we must always keep in mind that there may have been a similar "behind-the-scenes" conversation regarding us. God has established the limits of our trial, but we just do not know what those limits are!

What we as Christian's experience is not generally time and chance. The devil does not "sneak up" while God's back is turned. God is involved in every test that we undergo, and He has established preset limits beyond which Satan cannot go. Neither the duration nor the intensity of the trial is completely open-ended. Ultimately, God is in charge!

Lesson 3 — Seek Growth, Not Justification

This is perhaps one of the hardest lessons to keep in mind. Job wanted God to justify and defend him in the eyes of his friends. People ridiculed him (Job 30:1 & 9) and that can be hard to take. When Elihu began to answer Job on behalf of God in chapters 32 through 37, he pointed out that Job had been wrongly focused during much of his trial. In Job 33:12–22, Elihu explains that God instructs and chastens in various ways. God has His reasons for how He deals with us. And sometimes they are beyond our understanding.

Job was so certain of his innocence and of the injustice of his afflictions that for a long time he was unable to see beyond that. He tried to defend himself from the false conclusions of his friends and in so doing was unable to see areas of needed growth in his life.

Again, God has reasons for allowing whatever happens — though we are often at a loss to understand what they are. In our trials and tests, James encourages us to ask God for wisdom (James 1:5). If we do so in faith, He will surely give it. Whatever the trial or test, there is always growth that can be achieved. Even Jesus Christ Himself learned by the things He suffered (Hebrews 5:8). God wants us to grow. Therefore, we must undergo periodic pruning to stimulate that growth (John 15:2).

Lesson 4 — The "Why" Often Proves Confusing and Hard to Understand

Humanly, we like everything to be neatly organized. We want the world and the events in it to make sense. But in trying to explain everything we sometimes miss the point. This is the way it was for Job's friends.

The first of Job's friends to speak was Eliphaz. He declared, "Remember, I pray thee, who ever perished, being innocent? or where were the righteous cut off? ⁸ Even as I have seen, they that plow iniquity, and sow wickedness, reap the same." **(4:7–8)**. Eliphaz, Bildad and Zophar, Job's three friends, were all sure that Job must have had some secret sin at the root of his newfound troubles. They "knew" there had to be a reason. So, they badgered poor Job to confess this suspected secret sin.

Job knew there was no great hidden scandal in his life engendering his trials. He was defensive in the face of his accusers, but he also wondered — "Why?" One of the difficult things for us to accept is that many of the sufferings we go through simply cannot be neatly categorized. The "why" is often elusive and baffling. Bad things do not only happen to bad people. Job recognized that many times the wicked live to reach old age and even appear to prosper **(21:7–13)**. There are many "why's" that we will never know in this life. Acceptance that the "why" may prove elusive sets the stage for a fifth vital lesson from the book of Job.

Lesson 5 — Trust in the Face of Anguish and Pain

Job was in despair. His whole life had been turned upside down. He had lost his wealth and his loved ones in a series of sudden calamities. Now his health is gone too. Why? Job was deeply frustrated because he could not make sense out of his trials. Yet in the depths of perplexity and despair he made one of the most profound declarations of faith recorded in the Bible: "Though He slay me, yet will I trust Him" (13:15).

In Job 19 we read the words of anguish that poured from Job's lips. 6 Know now that God hath overthrown me, and hath compassed me with his net.... 8 He hath fenced up my way that I cannot pass, and he hath set darkness in my paths.... 14 My kinsfolk have failed, and my familiar friends have forgotten me.... 17 My breath is strange to my wife, though I intreated for the children's sake of mine own body. (vv. 6, 8, 14, 17).

Yet even at this low point of anguish and bewilderment Job declares his heartfelt trust in God. 25 For I know that my redeemer liveth, and that he shall stand at the latter day upon the earth: 26 And though after my skin worms destroy this body, yet in my flesh shall I see God: 27 Whom I shall see for myself, and mine eyes shall behold, and not another; though my reins be consumed within me. (Job 19:25–27).

Job understood and had a revelation of the truth of the resurrection. "If a man die, shall he live again?" Job asked. He went on to record the divinely inspired answer. "All the days of my appointed time I will wait, till my change come (14:14). Job knew that God would call and that he would answer and come forth from the grave, because God would have a desire to the work of His hands (v. 15).

It is relatively easy to trust God when things are going the way we like them. When the world around us makes sense, it is easy to believe God is in charge. But what about when things turn upside down and inside out? It is during such perplexity and anguish that faith in God is most needed.

One of the things Satan never understood about Job was his motive. Satan thought Job only served God because it was to his advantage here and now. He was convinced that if God removed blessings and protection, Job would curse and revile Him. But that was not true. Job loved God and served Him out of sincere devotion. He trusted God even when he was feeling abandoned. This lesson of steadfast trust is one of the most important aspects of character growth that we can gain from any trial.

Lesson 6 – God Will Ultimately Reward both Good and Evil

Life can often seem unfair. There are those who make no pretense of serving God and yet they seem to be doing well. There are others who are genuinely trying, but they are experiencing many difficulties and setbacks. What we must keep in mind is that this life is temporary.

Job noticed that there were wicked men whose "9houses are safe from fear, neither is the rod of God upon them 10Their bull gendereth, and faileth not; their cow calveth, and casteth not her calf." (21:9–10). Yet he realized that was not the end of the story.

In verse 30 of the same chapter, Job said, "That the wicked is reserved to the day of destruction? they shall be brought forth to the day of wrath." Even though it may seem that life is not fair, God is a God of justice.

Ultimately, it is in the resurrection that God will reward the righteous and punish the wicked. However, there are many times when even in this life events can make a sudden shift. The conclusion of the book of Job reveals, "So the Lord blessed the latter end of Job more than his beginning:" **(42:12).** In the long run, there are blessings for obedience — entrance into the Kingdom of God is the greatest of all blessings — and curses for disobedience.

Lesson 7 — We Emerge and Grow When We Learn What God Is Teaching

God is the great Teacher who is preparing us for a role in His Kingdom and He insists that we learn our lessons properly. It was only when Job began coming to grips with the lessons that God wanted Him to learn that he began emerging from his period of great trial.

God focuses on the bottom line. He wants us to become like Him. Job was an exemplary man, but he had a flaw. The Scriptures say Job's problem was that "he was righteous in his own eyes and that "he justified himself rather than God" **(32:1–2).** Ultimately Job emerged with a far deeper understanding of the Almighty as well as a deeper understanding of himself and his own human nature. We see this in **Job 42:5-6** where he states "I have heard of thee by the hearing of the ear, but now mine eye seeth thee. Therefore I abhor myself, and repent in dust and ashes," Job told God **(Job 42:6).**

A vital lesson that all of us must learn to please God and to begin emerging from a trial is that of mercy and forgiveness. Job's friends were miserable comforters. Regardless of their motives, they were a great part of Job's trial. Yet notice the turning point when Job began to emerge from his great adversity. 'And the Lord restored Job's losses when he prayed for his friends" **(Job 42:10).**

Conclusion

Job came to really know God deeply, not simply to know about Him. He became a far more humble and compassionate man with an even more steadfast trust because of what he went through. Learning these lessons was the key to his coming out of the dark trials of life and into the sunlight of God's favor and grace once again.

CHAPTER 13

Letting Go of the Past and Pressing Forward to the Future

(JOHN 2:5)

Introduction

The life and ministry of the apostle Paul was controlled by one supreme objective, and it is to this that he refers in Philippians 3:13-14 — "But one thing I do. Forgetting what is behind and straining towards what is ahead, I press on towards the goal for the prize of the upward call of God in Christ Jesus...." Paul is using an illustration from the realm of athletics. He pictures a Greek runner.

As he runs along the prescribed course he forgets all thoughts of past failures, and he strains every nerve in an effort of tremendous concentration on reaching his goal; his one and only concern is to win the race. Likewise, if we are to succeed in the race of life we must very deliberately "*forget*", and very deliberately "*press on*". To forget in Greek is (epilanthanomai) — *neglecting, no longer caring for; forgotten, given over to oblivion, i.e. uncared for.* To receive something new we must let go of something old. Old habits, old ways of doing things, old sins, old friends. To press on in the Greek is *diōkō* — *to pursue (in a hostile manner), to run swiftly in order to catch a person or thing, to run after.*

THINGS WHICH ARE BEHIND WHICH
WE SHOULD FORGET

A. We must confess, forsake and forget our past sins.
That is, if we have truly repented, confessed and forsaken them (**Proverbs 28:13** *He who covers his sins will not prosper. But whoever confesses and forsakes them will have mercy.*), then we must forget them. If we have confessed and renounced our sin, God has forgiven it and forgotten it (1 John 1:9 and compare Psalm 103:12; Isaiah 44:22; Micah 7:19 and Hebrews 10:17). If God has forgotten our sins, we must do the same, otherwise the memory of them will hinder us.

B. We must forget our past failures.
2 Corinthians 5:17, *Therefore, if anyone is in Christ, he is a new creation. The old has passed away; behold, the new has come.* This is not easy, but if we are constantly dwelling upon our failures and reviving the memory of them, we shall find that our peace is destroyed, our progress is impeded, and our usefulness is limited. Some people are always filled with regret over what might have been. *"Don't cry over spilt milk!"* Get another glass.

C. We must forget our past pleasures.
The Children of Israel failed just here, and frequently we read of them crying for the abundance of food and water which they had had in Egypt –– look up Numbers 11:5-6

(⁵ We remember the fish which we ate freely in Egypt, the cucumbers, the melons, the leeks, the onions, and the garlic; ⁶but now our whole being is dried up; there is nothing at all except this manna before our eyes!"); 20:5 and 21:5. To be engrossed with the past advantages of Egypt is to fail to realize the value of God's present miraculous provision.

D. We must forget our past unhappy experiences.

Have we lost a fortune? Forget it! -- thinking of it cannot bring it back. Has someone let us down? Forget it! -- to keep reviving the memory of the experience will cause resentment, and this will do far more harm to ourselves than to anyone else.

E. We must forget our past blessings.

Yesterday's provision will not suffice for today's demands. The Lord's provision is "new every morning" **Lamentations 3:22-23** — Through the Lord's mercies we are not consumed, Because His compassions fail not. 23) They are new every morning; Great is Your faithfulness.

F. We must forget the sins and the failures of others.

(Matthew 18:21-22) — Then Peter came up and said to him, "Lord, how often will my brother sin against me, and I forgive him? As many as seven times?" ²²Jesus said to him, "I do not say to you seven times, but seventy-seven times. This needs to be said, for we so easily remember the shortcomings of other people. If we have been wronged, we must forgive and we must forget. Do not say, "I can't!" You can! Otherwise, God will not forgive our sins.

THINGS AHEAD WHICH WE MUST STRIVE TO ATTAIN

We must press on to perfection.

The first part of verse 12 tells us this, and the word "perfect" means "spiritually mature", not sinless or faultless. Here the need for growth is implied -- look up Hebrews 6:1, "Therefore let us leave the elementary teachings about Christ and go on to maturity, not laying again the foundation of repentance from dead works, and of faith in God." To grow we must feed upon the Word of God; we must regularly engage in prayer and have sufficient work to do in the Lord's vineyard.

We must press on to take hold of the purpose for which God has taken hold of us.

The second part of verse 12 tells us this. God's general purpose for us is indicated in Romans 8:28-30, And we know that God causes all things to work together for good to those who love God, to those who are called according to His purpose. [29] For those whom He foreknew, He also predestined to become conformed to the image of His Son, so that He would be the firstborn among many brethren; [30] and these whom He predestined, He also called; and these whom He called, He also justified; and these whom He justified, He also glorified. But He has a particular purpose for every one of us -- a life plan. Have you discovered God's plan for your life and are you pressing on? — look up Acts 9:6 and make Paul's question your question every day! This was Paul's question to Jesus on the road to Damascus, "Lord, what would You have me to do."

We must press on with deep concern to win the lost.

This surely should be our attitude to those mentioned in verses 18-19. As we hurry on to the time of the Lord's coming, which will mean glory for us and gloom for the lost, we should be burdened to win souls — look up 2 Peter 3:10-12. But the day of the Lord will come as a thief in the night; in the which the heavens shall pass away with a great noise, and the elements shall melt with fervent heat, the earth also and the works that are therein shall be burned up. [11] Seeing then that all these things shall be dissolved, what manner of persons ought ye to be in all holy conversation and godliness, [12] Looking for and hasting unto the coming of the day of God, wherein the heavens being on fire shall be dissolved, and the elements shall melt with fervent heat?

Keep Walking in the Light of God's Word

When we choose to forgive others, forget the past and its failures, forget our old person, walk in the newness of life then we will walk in God's light and His favor and grace will be upon our lives. We will be as lights in a dark world showing others the way to Christ and His salvation. (Ephesians 5:6-11) Let no man deceive you with vain words: for because of these things cometh the wrath of God upon the children of disobedience. [7] Be not ye therefore partakers with them. [8] For ye were sometimes darkness, but now are ye light in the Lord: walk as children of light: [9] (For the fruit of the Spirit is in all goodness and righteousness and truth;) [10] Proving what is acceptable unto the Lord. [11] And have no fellowship with the unfruitful works of darkness, but rather reprove them.

REASONS WE TO DO "THIS ONE THING", WHICH CONSISTS OF "FORGETTING WHAT IS BEHIND, AND STRAINING TOWARD WHAT IS AHEAD

Because we are citizens of Heaven. Heaven is our home; our names are written there (Luke 10:20), and many who are members of God's family are already there (Ephesians 3:15).

Because the Lord is coming to take us Home. What an incentive this is to holy living (1 John 1:3) and to patient endurance! (Romans 8:25)

Because we shall exchange these old bodies for new ones. This is what verse 21 says. We shall have a body just like His body –- look up 1 Corinthians 15:20 and 23.

Because the Prize Day is coming. Verse 14 tells us this, and it reminds us that we shall all appear before the Judgment Seat of Christ, to be rewarded or to suffer loss –- look up Romans 14:12; 1 Corinthians 3:12-15 and 2 Corinthians 5:10.

Personal Testimony of Letting Go

There came a time in my life where I had to let go of the old person that I was. Despite all the hurts and disappointments I realized I needed to begin to live a new life in Christ. (II Corinthians 5:17) I had to let go of that old negative attitude, bitterness and unforgiveness which I was raised in. I learned from my new family, the family of God, the church on how to live this new life.

Conclusion

For to every faithful servant shall it be granted at the day of final judgment, to enter into the joy of his Lord, Matthew 25:23; to sit down with him on his throne, as he overcame and is set down with his Father on his throne; and to inherit all things, even all that God has and is. So let us run this race forgetting those things which are past and pressing forward to the high calling in Christ Jesus.

CHAPTER 14

The Story Of Joseph

(GENESIS 37)

Introduction

The story of Joseph is a truly remarkable story of how the promises and hand of God can keep a man in the most difficult of circumstances. It shows how the very things of life that work against us, with God on our side are working for our good. God does not see life as we see it. We see the immediate circumstances, but God sees the beginning from the end. It is a faith walk we have been called into. The story of Joseph has many life lessons that we can benefit from in our walk of faith.

Summary of the Life of Joseph

The Bible Story of Joseph, from the Book of Genesis, is one of heroic redemption and forgiveness. Joseph was the most loved son of his father, Israel, given the famous robe of many colors. When Joseph reported having dreams of his brothers, and even the stars and moon, bowing before him, their jealousy of Joseph grew into action. The brothers sold him into slavery to a traveling caravan of Ishmaelites who took him to Egypt and sold him to Potiphar, the captain of Pharaoh's guard.

In Egypt, the Lord's presence with Joseph enables him to find favor with Potiphar and the keeper of the prison. With God's help, Joseph interprets the dreams of two prisoners, predicting that one of them will be reinstated but the other put to death. Joseph then interprets the dreams of the Pharaoh, which anticipate seven years of plenty followed by seven years of famine. Pharaoh recognizes Joseph's God-given ability and prompts his promotion to the chief administrator of Egypt.

Shortage of food in Canaan forces Jacob to send his sons to buy grains from the Egyptians. Benjamin, Joseph's younger brother remains at home as Jacob fears of losing him, as he did Joseph. When Joseph finally encounters his brothers again, he deliberately conceals his identity. He accuses them of being spies and tells them to return with Benjamin or he will not sell them grain. The ongoing famine forces Jacob to reluctantly send his sons back to Egypt with Benjamin, and they are unexpectedly invited to dine at Joseph's house. Joseph then tests the character of his brothers by placing a silver cup in the sack of Benjamin and falsely accusing him of theft.

When Judah offers to stay in place of Benjamin, Joseph knows that his character has changed and reveals that he is their brother. Joseph explains they need not feel guilty for betraying him as it was God's plan for him to be in Egypt to preserve his family. He told them to bring their father and his entire household into Egypt to live in the province of Goshen because there were five more years of famine left. Joseph supplied them Egyptian transport wagons, new garments, silver, and twenty additional donkeys carrying provisions for the journey. Jacob is then joyously reunited with his son Joseph.

Reading of Genesis 37: 1-36

And Jacob dwelt in the land wherein his father was a stranger, in the land of Canaan. ² These are the generations of Jacob. Joseph, being seventeen years old, was feeding the flock with his brethren; and the lad was with the sons of Bilhah, and with the sons of Zilpah, his father's wives: and Joseph brought unto his father their evil report.

³ Now Israel loved Joseph more than all his children, because he was the son of his old age: and he made him a coat of many colours. ⁴ And when his brethren saw that their father loved him more than all his brethren, they hated him, and could not speak peaceably unto him.

⁵ And Joseph dreamed a dream, and he told it his brethren: and they hated him yet the more. ⁶ And he said unto them, Hear, I pray you, this dream which I have dreamed: ⁷ For, behold, we were binding sheaves in the field, and, lo, my sheaf arose, and also stood upright; and, behold, your sheaves stood round about, and made obeisance to my sheaf.

⁸ And his brethren said to him, Shalt thou indeed reign over us? or shalt thou indeed have dominion over us? And they hated him yet the more for his dreams, and for his words.

⁹ And he dreamed yet another dream, and told it his brethren, and said, Behold, I have dreamed a dream more; and, behold, the sun and the moon and the eleven stars made obeisance to me. ¹⁰ And he told it to his father, and to his brethren: and his father rebuked him, and said unto him, What is this dream that thou hast dreamed? Shall I and thy mother and thy brethren indeed come to bow down ourselves to thee to the earth? ¹¹ And his brethren envied him; but his father observed the saying. ¹² And his brethren went to feed their father's flock in Shechem.

¹³ And Israel said unto Joseph, Do not thy brethren feed the flock in Shechem? come, and I will send thee unto them. And he said to him, Here am I.

¹⁴ And he said to him, Go, I pray thee, see whether it be well with thy brethren, and well with the flocks; and bring me word again. So he sent him out of the vale of Hebron, and he came to Shechem. ¹⁵ And a certain man found him, and, behold, he was wandering in the field: and the man asked him, saying, What seekest thou?

¹⁶ And he said, I seek my brethren: tell me, I pray thee, where they feed their flocks. ¹⁷ And the man said, They are departed hence; for I heard them say, Let us go to Dothan. And Joseph went after his brethren, and found them in Dothan.

¹⁸ And when they saw him afar off, even before he came near unto them, they conspired against him to slay him.

¹⁹ And they said one to another, Behold, this dreamer cometh. ²⁰ Come now therefore, and let us slay him, and cast him into some pit, and we will say, Some evil beast hath devoured him: and we shall see what will become of his dreams.

²¹ And Reuben heard it, and he delivered him out of their hands; and said, Let us not kill him.

²² And Reuben said unto them, Shed no blood, but cast him into this pit that is in the wilderness, and lay no hand upon him; that he might rid him out of their hands, to deliver him to his father again.

²³ And it came to pass, when Joseph was come unto his brethren, that they stript Joseph out of his coat, his coat of many colours that was on him;

²⁴ And they took him, and cast him into a pit: and the pit was empty, there was no water in it. ²⁵ And they sat down to eat bread: and they lifted up their eyes and looked, and, behold, a company of Ishmeelites came from Gilead with their camels bearing spicery and balm and myrrh, going to carry it down to Egypt.

²⁶ And Judah said unto his brethren, What profit is it if we slay our brother, and conceal his blood? ²⁷ Come, and let us sell him to the Ishmeelites, and let not our hand be upon him; for he is our brother and our flesh. And his brethren were content.

²⁸ Then there passed by Midianites merchantmen; and they drew and lifted up Joseph out of the pit, and sold Joseph to the Ishmeelites for twenty pieces of silver: and they brought Joseph into Egypt.

²⁹ And Reuben returned unto the pit; and, behold, Joseph was not in the pit; and he rent his clothes. ³⁰ And he returned unto his brethren, and said, The child is not; and I, whither shall I go?

³¹ And they took Joseph's coat, and killed a kid of the goats, and dipped the coat in the blood; ³² And they sent the coat of

many colours, and they brought it to their father; and said, This have we found: know now whether it be thy son's coat or no.

³³ And he knew it, and said, It is my son's coat; an evil beast hath devoured him; Joseph is without doubt rent in pieces. ³⁴ And Jacob rent his clothes, and put sackcloth upon his loins, and mourned for his son many days.

³⁵ And all his sons and all his daughters rose up to comfort him; but he refused to be comforted; and he said, For I will go down into the grave unto my son mourning. Thus his father wept for him.

³⁶ And the Midianites sold him into Egypt unto Potiphar, an officer of Pharaoh's, and captain of the guard.

Practical Lessons

Joseph gives a bad report about his other brother's actions which puts him in an estranged relationship with them. *We see the goodness of Joseph and the evil behavior of his brothers and Joseph wanting to see that corrected for good purposes. The bible states that even a child is known by his behavior.*

Jacob was favored by his father and his other sons hated Joseph for it. *As a parent we need to guard against favoritism, it can create discord and jealousy.*

We see the evil heart of his brothers and how the bible states the evil hate the good. *They strip him of his coat and want* to kill him, but Reuben speaks up for him and they throw him in a pit. God loves us but in hell the demons hate us.

Joseph is sold as a slave to traveling merchantmen for 20 pieces of silver. *In today's economy, the denomination of the silver coins was called shekels. Coins containing that amount of silver (about the size of an American silver dollar) would be* **worth** *about $10* **today.** *Thus the 20 pieces would be* **worth** *about $200* **today.**

Deception given to Jacob's father about Joseph being killed by a beast. *This will lead him into great grief and still because of the evil hearts of his sons they would not tell him the truth, but all along this was God's plan in getting Joseph in a great position later.*

Jacob again is sold by the merchants going into Egypt. *He was sold to Potiphar, an officer of Pharaoh's, and captain of the guard. Again, we see God skillfully directing Joseph's path to one day be second in command to Pharaoh.*

We need to remember that present circumstances are not always accurate in determining our future. *But God does take and use them to develop us for our future in work and ministry.*

Conclusion

Life can become very complex at times. It is trust and faith in God's promises to us and His hand over our lives that keep us. In this lesson of Joseph's life, we can see how with God the things that seem to work against us, are actually working for us. Let us end with this verse in *Romans 8:28 "And we know that all things work together for good to them that love God, to them who are the called, according to his purpose."*

CHAPTER 15

Love Your Enemies

(MATTHEW 5:43-48)

Introduction

Jesus is the essence of Love. To behold Jesus is to behold the perfect example of God's love. There is a saying that goes like this, *"we become what we behold."* We can love our enemies only when the love of God is shed abroad in our hearts by the Holy Spirit. When we have been truly born again and the love of God has touched and healed our heart, mind and spirit can we be free to love others. If we want to make an impact in the lives of others around us then let us choose to follow our Lord in His command to love, not just our neighbor, but even our enemies.

Scripture Reading
Matthew 5:43-48

Ye have heard that it hath been said, Thou shalt love thy neighbour, and hate thine enemy.

44 But I say unto you, Love your enemies, bless them that curse you, do good to them that hate you, and pray for them which despitefully use you, and persecute you;

45 That ye may be the children of your Father which is in

heaven: for he maketh his sun to rise on the evil and on the good, and sendeth rain on the just and on the unjust.

⁴⁶ For if ye love them which love you, what reward have ye? do not even the publicans the same?

⁴⁷ And if ye salute your brethren only, what do ye more than others? do not even the publicans so?

⁴⁸ Be ye therefore perfect, even as your Father which is in heaven is perfect.

Commentary on Matthew 5:43-48

The Jewish teachers by neighbor understood only those who were of their own country, nation, and religion, whom they were pleased to look upon as their friends. The Lord Jesus teaches that we must do all the real kindness we can to all, especially to their souls. We must pray for them. While many will render good for good, we must render good for evil; and this will speak a nobler principle than most men act by. Others salute their brethren, and embrace those of their own party, and ways, and opinions, but we must not so confine our respect. It is the duty of Christians to desire, and aim at, and press towards perfection in grace and holiness. And therein we must study to conform ourselves to the example of our heavenly Father, 1ˢᵗ Peter 1:15-16. Surely more is to be expected from the followers of Christ than from others; surely more will be found in them than in others. Let us beg God to enable us to prove ourselves, His children.

The Old Testament of precept of love is found in **Lev.19:18**, but hatred of one's enemies was added by the Pharisees. Love is not a matter of sentiment or feeling but shows itself in practical ways such as blessing others, praying for them and to both friend and enemy. Just like God who sends the rain on both the just and unjust so we must extend love toward all. In our Lord's command to be perfect, it is not about us having a flawless moral character but an inclusive love that seeks for the good of all. Instead of being like sinners who only love those who love them we are to be like our heavenly Father loving those who do not love us.

Personal Experience

We are naturally drawn to those who like us, and we like them. I can remember an experience on a job site where I was harassed everyday by a coworker. Later I found out that the reason he had such a hate for me was that I was hired into a position that he wanted. It tested my spirituality in ways I had never been tested. I went from anger to frustration to prayer to humility to victory. When I quit reacting to the insults and remained calm and undisturbed (only by the grace of God) that my enemy begin to back away. Later I had an opportunity to witness both to him and my boss as my deliverance was at hand when I was being laid off. It was a day of rejoicing.

Conclusion

If we will dare to follow our Lord's command to love our enemies, which can even be those of our own family as well as coworkers and strangers, we will see the divine hand of God move in their lives. It will impact and bring transformation into lives that need it most, which are the lost, the hurting, and the unlovable. Our own lives will change in ways that will cause us to become more like our Lord's likeness, who not only loved the sinner but gave his life on the cross for all of mankind that they might be saved.

CHAPTER 16

Overcome Evil With Good

(ROMANS 12:21)

Introduction

The word overcome in the greek is *nikáō* (from 3529 /*níkŏ*, "victory") — properly, *conquer* (overcome); " 'to carry off the victory, come off victorious.' The verb implies a battle". It also menas to seize , bind or restrain is

Key Scripture

Romans 12: 21 — Do not be overcome by evil but overcome evil with good.

Admonitions From Scripture on
Overcoming Evil with Good

Romans 12:9-21

Let love be without dissimulation. Abhor that which is evil; cleave to that which is good.

¹⁰ Be kindly affectioned one to another with brotherly love; in honour preferring one another;

[11] Not slothful in business; fervent in spirit; serving the Lord;

[12] Rejoicing in hope; patient in tribulation; continuing instant in prayer;

[13] Distributing to the necessity of saints; given to hospitality.

[14] Bless them which persecute you: bless, and curse not.

[15] Rejoice with them that do rejoice, and weep with them that weep.

[16] Be of the same mind one toward another. Mind not high things, but condescend to men of low estate. Be not wise in your own conceits.

[17] Recompense to no man evil for evil. Provide things honest in the sight of all men.

[18] If it be possible, as much as lieth in you, live peaceably with all men.

[19] Dearly beloved, avenge not yourselves, but rather give place unto wrath: for it is written, VENGEANCE IS MINE; I WILL REPAY, SAITH THE LORD.

[20] THEREFORE IF THINE ENEMY HUNGER, FEED HIM; IF HE THIRST, GIVE HIM DRINK: FOR IN SO DOING THOU SHALT HEAP COALS OF FIRE ON HIS HEAD.

[21] Be not overcome of evil, but overcome evil with good.

A New Life

How is the new life that we live with Christ different from the life we lived before the new birth? How is the path different? The path is different because it is the path of discipleship, of following Jesus. As we follow Jesus, we start to "look" more and more like

Him; and as we look more like him, we look less like the world. Instead of being led by our emotions, the world, the flesh or our enemy the devil we are spirit led.

Principles Of Losing Our Lives to Save It

A. The Physical and Spiritual Life

The Scriptures teach, and I think every human being is at least aware of the fact that we are more than the sum of our body parts. There is the physical, outer part of us, that which the Bible calls "temporal", and the spiritual, inner person which the Bible says is "eternal" (that is, without end).

There is not only this life "under the sun (Ecclesiastes 1:3), but at death the dust will return to the earth as it was, and the spirit will return to God who gave it (Ecclesiastes 12:7) Only when one recognizes the importance of the eternal, unseen part of the human being (our spirit) will this principle make sense... only to those spiritually minded or born again. Some things only benefit us in this life, but better things benefit us in both this life and the next. Paul said, ...For bodily exercise profiteth little: but godliness is profitable unto all things, having promise of the life that now is, and of that which is to come. (1 Timothy 4:8). The question we all want an answer to is, how can we get the best out of both worlds? And are we wise enough to realize that the eternal riches of the next world are worth more than the temporary riches of this world?

B. Giving God First Place

When temporary things become less important and eternal things become more important to us, then we will begin to grasp the meaning of Jesus' statement. Faith puts God first because it believes His promises and assurances. It is the conviction of things not yet seen. But just because they have not yet been seen does not mean they are not of tremendous value already. Those things for which we hope to instill within us a joy and, if our faith is strong enough, even exultation that we have put God first. We will think of ourselves as rich and blessed, though outwardly we may not seem so. It is as Jesus Himself said to the church at Smyrna, I know thy works, and tribulation, and poverty, (but thou art rich) ... (Revelation 2:9) They were rich in good works toward God.

C. We Need to be Liberal

With our blessings, we could be building bigger barns (as Jesus described it in one of His parables-Luke 12:16-22) when greater happiness could be had by giving up some of that in favor of spiritual pursuits or kingdom matters. The carnal man has appraised his life and put a higher value on physical things than on the spiritual. This will not result in the depth of joy and confident strength possible in this life and will result in complete and utter tragedy in the life to come (**Romans 8:5-9; 1 Corinthians 2:14-16**) when he leaves this life to face judgment for selfish living instead of giving to God's work and kingdom.

D. Laying Hold of Life Indeed

Jesus had predicted that He would be put to death and said that the apostles would face similar treatment. When Peter objected to the idea that Jesus would die, Jesus responded For whoever wishes to save his life will lose it; but whoever loses his life for my sake will find it. To the apostles, as well as all faithful disciples, we must face the fact that the world expects us to renounce Jesus, or at least reject His teachings, to be acceptable, to be politically correct, to be popular, or sometimes, even to stay alive.

But if one does renounce Christ, or even merely ignore Him and His will, the things he will have saved will be next to valueless in the very near future. But if one will go so far as to lose his life rather than deny the Lord, he will find what life really is (1 Timothy 6:18, 19) That they do good, that they be rich in good works, ready to distribute, willing to communicate; [19] Laying up in store for themselves a good foundation against the time to come, that they may lay hold on eternal life.

E. Being Led By The Spirit

The Bible states in Romans 8:13, 14 — For if ye live after the flesh, ye shall die: but if ye through the Spirit do mortify the deeds of the body, ye shall live. [14] For as many as are led by the Spirit of God, they are the sons of God.

Comment:

To be led we must be willing to give up our right to be in control. We must be willing to follow the Lord and be open to the nudging or leading of the Holy Spirit in our lives. Not be concerned with appearance, political views, but being obedient and pleasing Him.

F. Losing the Temporal to Gain the Eternal

We must be willing to lose the temporal things of life, if need be, that we may faithfully and loyally follow Christ. It might involve losing comfort or physical security. It might mean forgoing something pleasurable or some source of momentary happiness. It might cost us acceptance with family, friends or associates. It might cost us physical wealth. These are the things of this life. We must put following Christ, above them all. The Christian never gives up anything for Jesus' sake without gaining something better. And no one reaching heaven will ever be disappointed.

Example of Losing to Gain

I was raised in a very close-knit family as a young man growing up. When I became a Christian, I noticed that changed. To this day I see more and more how I am excluded from certain family functions. I know I have lost that close relationship with my family only to have gained more brothers and sisters in the faith. God is always faithful; what we lose He replaces it with even better.

Conclusion

Being a disciple of Jesus has many challenges and also wonderful benefits. And, we are only at the beginning. In the words of Jesus in Mark 10:29-30 — And Jesus answered and said, Verily I say unto you, There is no man that hath left house, or brethren, or sisters, or father, or mother, or wife, or children, or lands, for my sake, and the gospel's, [30] But he shall receive an hundredfold now in this time, houses, and brethren, and sisters, and mothers, and children, and lands, with persecutions; and in the world to come eternal life.

We can only imagine what glories will be in the world to come, as one hymn suggests, we exult as the ages roll on. We may lose our lives, plans, goals, relationships, even physical life but in the end, we will save them and heaven will be our home and then we will begin to really live in the presence of our Lord Jesus Christ forever.

CHAPTER 17

God Has A Purpose For Allowing Adversity In Our Lives

(1 PETER 1:6-7)

Adversity does have its benefits. *"People who are never challenged by life don't have the opportunity to learn how to overcome adversity, which enables them to develop coping strategies, identify who the important members of their social network are, and feel competent after they make it through,"* says Roxane Cohen Silver, PhD, the University of California, Irvine, psychologist. James the Apostle recommended a similar response to troubles and adversity: *"My brethren,* **count it all joy when ye fall into divers temptations***, knowing this, that the trying of your faith worketh patience. But let patience have her perfect work, that ye may be perfect and entire, wanting nothing"* (James 1:2–4). If we submit to God as Joseph and other men and women did, God can and will use adversity to not only test us but strengthen us and eventually lead us to His divine purposes for our lives.

Definition of Adversity: Greek definition — kakoucheo — to ill-treat. to maltreat, torment. Another greek word is peirasmos — an experiment, a trial, temptation

Webster's Revised Unabridged Dictionary — Opposition; misfortune; contrariety

Purposes of Adversity

Adversity gets our attention

When adversity comes, we are forced to face problems and pressures that are too big for us to resolve. In this way, God gets our attention. We can't continue to pursue our goals, tasks, and relationships in the same manner. We must stop and evaluate our situation, ask God for wisdom, obey His Word, and trust Him to bring the help we need. Sometimes we can be too comfortable and complacent yet go in the wrong direction. To redirect our path, God uses adversity. For example, the story of Elijah being fed by the ravens near a brook in a time of famine, until the brook dried up and the ravens fed him no more, it was time for him to move, God had a different plan.

Troubles point out our weaknesses and prompt us to rely on God in ways that we wouldn't unless we had significant needs. Christ's invitation to those who are weary becomes very attractive during trials: "Come unto me, all ye that labor and are heavy laden, and I will give you rest. Take my yoke upon you and learn of me; for I am meek and lowly in heart: and ye shall find rest unto your souls. For my yoke is easy, and my burden is light" (Matthew 11:28–30). Adversity is a classroom in which we can learn more of Christ and become more like Him.

As we come to God with our needs, our inward prayer should echo these words of the Psalmist: "Unto thee, O Lord, do I lift up my soul. O my God, I trust in thee: let me not be ashamed, let not mine enemies' triumph over me" (Psalm 25:1–2).

Adversity reminds us of our weaknesses

The Apostle Paul knew what it meant to live with adversity that would not go away. He learned to see the good that God intended to bring to his life through it and to rejoice in God's design. He wrote: "Lest I should be exalted above measure through the abundance of the revelations, there was given to me a thorn in the flesh, the messenger of Satan to buffet me, lest I should be exalted above measure. For this thing I besought the Lord thrice, that it might depart from me. And he said unto me, My grace is sufficient for thee: for my strength is made perfect in weakness. Most gladly therefore will I rather glory in my infirmities, that the power of Christ may rest upon me. Therefore, I take pleasure in infirmities, in reproaches, in necessities, in persecutions, in distresses for Christ's sake: for when I am weak, then am I strong" (II Corinthians 12:7–10).

As we accept our unchangeable features and embrace God's purposes for our difficulties, we will experience the power of Christ in our lives. We can trust God to care for us and to provide all that we need. "Like as a father pitieth his children, so the Lord pitieth them that fear him. For He knoweth our frame: he remembereth that we are dust" (Psalm 103:13–14).

Adversity motivates us to cry out to God

God responds to the cry of His children when they suffer. "The righteous cry, and the Lord heareth, and deliver them out of all their troubles" (**Psalm 34:17**).

• We are to cry out to God with our voice. "I cried unto the Lord with my voice, and He heard me out of his holy hill" (**Psalm 3:4**).

• We can cry out to God for mercy each day. "Be merciful unto me, O Lord: for I cry unto thee daily" (**Psalm 86:3**).

• We are to cry out to God in humility. ". . . He forgetteth not the cry of the humble" (**Psalm 9:12**).

• We are to cry out to God with a pure heart. "If I regard iniquity in my heart, the Lord will not hear me" (**Psalm 66:18**).

Adversity is an assurance of God's fatherly love and care

Wise discipline brings a child to maturity. Just as a loving father helps his children learn and grow through the discipline he carries out in their lives, so God uses adversity to help us grow in holiness and become more like Him. When we persevere through hardship, we have proof that we are God's children.

For whom the Lord loveth he chasteneth, and scourgeth every son whom he receiveth. If ye endure chastening, God dealeth with you as with sons; for what son is he whom the father chasteneth not? But if ye be without chastisement, whereof all are partakers, then are ye bastards, and not sons. Furthermore, we have had fathers of our flesh which corrected us, and we gave them reverence: shall we not much rather be in subjection unto the Father of spirits, and live?

For they verily for a few days chastened us after their own pleasure; but he, for our profit, that we might be partakers of his holiness. Now no chastening for the present seemeth to be joyous, but grievous: nevertheless, afterward it yieldeth the peaceable fruit of righteousness unto them which are exercised thereby. Wherefore lift up the hands which hang down, and the feeble knees; and make straight paths for your feet, lest that which is lame be turned out of the way; but let it rather be healed (Hebrews 12:6–13).

Adversity is Evidence of Spiritual Warfare

A Christian must be aware of the spiritual battle that rages between God and the enemy, Satan. Learn to recognize that sometimes adversity comes in the form of spiritual warfare through weariness, confusion, division, and spiritual oppression.

During these trials, do not become overwhelmed or yield to the temptation to give up. The Apostle Paul encourages us to be strong, courageous, and prepared to be good soldiers: "Put on the whole armor of God, that ye may be able to stand against the wiles of the devil. For we wrestle not against flesh and blood, but against principalities, against powers, against the rulers of the darkness of this world, against spiritual wickedness in high places. Wherefore take unto you the whole armor of God, that ye may be able to withstand in the evil day, and having done all, to stand.

Stand therefore, having your loins girt about with truth, and having on the breastplate of righteousness; and your feet shod with the preparation of the gospel of peace; above all, taking the shield of faith, wherewith ye shall be able to quench all the fiery darts of the wicked. And take the helmet of salvation, and the sword of the Spirit, which is the word of God: praying always with all prayer and supplication in the Spirit and watching thereunto with all perseverance and supplication for all saints" (Ephesians 6:11–18).

Adversity is God's Method of Purifying Our Faith

Faith is essential for living the Christian life, because the ways of God are opposite to the natural inclinations of man. Thus, adversity may come at the hand of those who mock God's principles, or it may come when we violate God's principles. In either case, adversity is designed to strengthen our faith.

". . . Now for a season, if need be, ye are in heaviness through manifold temptations: that the trial of your faith, being much more precious than of gold that perisheth, though it be tried with fire, might be found unto praise and honor and glory at the appearing of Jesus Christ" (1st Peter 1:6–7).

The development of patience is another benefit of having our faith purified by the fire of adversity. ". . . The trying of your faith worketh patience" (James 1:3). It is through faith and patience that we inherit the promises of God. Be ". . . followers of them who through faith and patience inherit the promises" (Hebrews 6:12).

Adversity Invites us to Experience the Power of God

One of the ultimate purposes of adversity is to cause us to desire more of Christ's power in our lives. Troubles reveal that on our own we can't live in a way that honors God. We need to rely on God and receive His grace.

Paul willingly suffered the loss of all things so that he might gain more of Christ and experience the power of Christ's resurrection. He said: "I count all things but loss for the excellency of the knowledge of Christ Jesus my Lord: for whom I have suffered the loss of all things, and do count them but dung, that I may win Christ, and be found in him, not having mine own righteousness, which is of the law, but that which is through the faith of Christ, the righteousness which is of God by faith: that I may know him, and the power of his resurrection, and the fellowship of his sufferings, being made conformable unto his death" (Philippians 3:8–10).

God works within the Christian in a mighty way, making him dead to sin and alive in Christ and enabling him to walk in the power of the Holy Spirit rather than according to fleshly desires. (See Romans 6–8.)

For the church of Ephesus, Paul prayed "that the God of our Lord Jesus Christ, the Father of glory, may give unto you the spirit of wisdom and revelation in the knowledge of him: the eyes of your understanding being enlightened; that ye may know what is the hope of his calling, and what [are] the riches of the glory of his inheritance in the saints, and what is the exceeding greatness of his power to us-ward who believe, according to the working of his mighty power, which he wrought in Christ, when he raised him from the dead, and set him at his own right hand in the heavenly places, far above all principality, and power, and might, and dominion, and every name that is named, not only in this world, but also in that which is to come: and hath put all things under his feet, and gave him to be the head over all things to the church, which is his body, the fullness of him that filleth all in all" (Ephesians 1:17–23).

Adversity Prepares Us to Comfort Others

One of the most valuable results of adversity is that through it we receive God's comfort, which we are then able to share with others who face similar troubles. "Blessed be God, even the Father of our Lord Jesus Christ, the Father of mercies, and the God of all comfort; Who comforteth us in all our tribulation, that we may be able to comfort them which are in any trouble, by the comfort wherewith we ourselves are comforted of God. For as the sufferings of Christ abound in us, so our consolation also aboundeth by Christ." (II Corinthians 1:3–5).

Suffering brings pain, but it is not an end in itself. [8] "We are troubled on every side, yet not distressed; we are perplexed, but not in despair; [9] persecuted, but not forsaken; cast down, but not destroyed; [10] always bearing about in the body the dying of the Lord Jesus, that the life also of Jesus might be made manifest in our body. . . [12] So then death worketh in us, but life in you. . . [16] For which because we faint not; but though our outward man perishes, yet the inward man is renewed day by day" (II Corinthians 4:8-10, 12 & 16).

Adversity Does Not Mean We Are Not in God's Will

Story of David and how God used adversity. David was minding his own business one day, tending sheep, when God called him to be a king. Talk about a God moment. He didn't ask to be king, but God said he was the one. He turned out to be a great king. Imagine that? God made a good pick! David had a heart modeled after God's, according to the Bible. So, since God had chosen to bless David in such a way, why do we later find Saul trying to kill David? In fact, for some time Saul chased David. David hid out, all alone, which is the setting we find him in during the writings of many of the Psalms. David was God's choice for king and yet he was placed in incredible adversity.

What does this tell us? I think it says to me that sometimes God's will for us will find us in the middle of trials in life. That's right. His will for our lives. More importantly, I am learning that I cannot determine whether I am in God's will, based on whether or not my life is peaceful. Just because I have trials in my life, doesn't mean I am not in the center of God's will for my life. I love how Alistair Begg once said it. *"We should not seek to confirm God's will by the absence of adversity."*

Biblical Characters Who Faced Great Trials

• Abraham who faced the trial of leaving his homeland, then the years of infertility.

- Moses wandered in the wilderness forty years.
- Joseph was sold into slavery.
- Ruth lost her husband.
- Nehemiah had to fight off enemies and intimidation.
- Daniel was thrown into a lion's den.
- John the Baptist was beheaded.
- Paul wrote some of his best work in prison.

All of these great servants of God faced persecution, heartache, and trials beyond most of our imaginations. Yet all of them, during the adversity, were right where God wanted them to be, in the center of His will. Yes, we would all like life to be peaceful. It is true that we can have inner peace and joy even in the middle of the storms of life. But God has not promised us a life free of problems. In fact, we can be perfectly within His will and still be facing adversity. It is often through the process of life's difficulties that God makes us more like Jesus, teaches us more about Him and ourselves. Trust Him, regardless of your circumstances! He is always working on a plan!

Six Ways to Stand up Today as Daniel Did in His Culture

1. Be faithful

Honor God and His word day in and day out as a reflection of His holiness. Daniel 2: 20-21

2. Be Gracious

Show gracious restraint and respect to authority even when our

Christian beliefs may conflict. (Daniel 6:3)

3. Be Steadfast

Trust in God and have unwavering faith and believe that He is in control, and He will deliver us into victory. (Daniel 6:22)

4. Be Strong

Ask God to give us the strength, yet humility to show God's message to our culture in truth with grace, love and compassion. (Daniel 2:28)

5. Be Consistent

Remember changing our society, our families, and enemies take time. Life is not a sprint but a marathon, stay consistent in your walk. (Daniel 1:21)

Conclusion

We need to learn to accept adversity and be open to God and learn these valuable lessons, He is trying to teach us. We also need to let it have its way in us developing our faith and trust and patience. God always has a good plan for our lives and adversity is just one of the tools He uses to prepare us in becoming more Christ-like and being used for His kingdom purposes.

CHAPTER 18

Overcoming Discouragement

(PHILIPPIANS 2:1-2)

Introduction

If faith is one of God's greatest weapons in our lives, then discouragement is one of Satan's greatest weapons against believers. How many believers have lost their salvation, backslidden and departed from the faith because of this merciless weapon. The bible states that Satan has come to steal, kill and destroy. Jesus has come to destroy the works of the devil.

Definition of Discouragement

Discouragement in the Greek — athumeo) — is defined as *I lose heart. I am despondent, am disheartened.* Webster defines it as *the act of making something less likely to happen or of making people less likely to do something: a feeling of having lost hope or confidence: something (such as a failure or difficulty) that discourages someone.*

Story of Discouragement Exodus 6:1-13

Then the LORD said unto Moses, Now shalt thou see what I will do to Pharaoh: for with a strong hand shall he let them go, and with a strong hand shall he drive them out of his land. ² And God spake unto Moses, and said unto him, I am the LORD: ³ And I appeared unto Abraham, unto Isaac, and unto Jacob, by the name of God Almighty, but by my name JEHOVAH was I not known to them. ⁴ And I have also established my covenant with them, to give them the land of Canaan, the land of their pilgrimage, wherein they were strangers.

⁵ And I have also heard the groaning of the children of Israel, whom the Egyptians keep in bondage; and I have remembered my covenant. ⁶ Wherefore say unto the children of Israel, I am the LORD, and I will bring you out from under the burdens of the Egyptians, and I will rid you out of their bondage, and I will redeem you with a stretched out arm, and with great judgments: ⁷ And I will take you to me for a people, and I will be to you a God: and ye shall know that I am the LORD your God, which bringeth you out from under the burdens of the Egyptians. ⁸ And I will bring you in unto the land, concerning the which I did swear to give it to Abraham, to Isaac, and to Jacob; and I will give it you for an heritage: I am the LORD.

⁹ And Moses spake so unto the children of Israel: but they hearkened not unto Moses for anguish of spirit, and for cruel bondage. ¹⁰ And the LORD spake unto Moses, saying, ¹¹ Go in, speak unto Pharaoh king of Egypt, that he let the children of Israel go out of his land. ¹² And Moses spake before the LORD, saying, Behold, the children of Israel have not hearkened unto me; how then shall Pharaoh hear me, who am of uncircumcised lips? ¹³ And the LORD spake unto Moses and unto Aaron, and gave them a

charge unto the children of Israel, and unto Pharaoh king of Egypt, to bring the children of Israel out of the land of Egypt.

My Comment:

We are most likely to prosper in attempts to glorify God, and to be useful to men, when we learn by experience that we can do nothing of ourselves; when our whole dependence is placed on him, and our only expectation is from him. Moses had been expecting what God would do; but now he shall see what he will do. God would now be known by his name Jehovah, that is, a God performing what he had promised, and finishing his own work. God intended their happiness: God said I will take you to me for a people, a peculiar people, and I will be to you a God.

More than this we need not ask, we cannot have, to make us happy but God. He intended his own glory: for He said, Ye shall know that I am the Lord. These good words, and comfortable words, should have revived the drooping Israelites, and have made them forget their misery; but they were so taken up with their troubles, that they did not heed God's promises. By indulging in discontent and worry, we deprive ourselves of the comfort we might have, both from God's word and from his providence, and go comfortless. It is at this point that we need to listen and take up the promises of God once again and do what He says.

My Comment:

God saw the end from the beginning. He had a plan in mind

and knew that the children of Israel would be delivered from Egyptian bondage to slavery by His mighty hand. He began to encourage Moses with what He was going to do and who He was and how He would take the children of Israel and be their God and they would be His people. Yet when Moses spoke these words of comfort and encouragement that they were still discouraged and despondent because they had been in cruel bondage and discouragement for so long that they would not listen to Moses.

Then God told Moses to tell Pharoah to let the children of Israel go. Moses then told God that even the children of Israel did not listen to him and asked why Pharoah should listen to him and especially since he was slow of speech. Yet in all this God still carried His plan out through Moses by encouraging him and giving him Aaron to speak for him. God doesn't view discouragement as we do, He continues His plans and purposes despite circumstances, He just asks us to do what He says, and He will do miracles.

Scriptures on Encouragement (Consolation)

Philippians 2:1-2 — If there be therefore any consolation in Christ, if any comfort of love, if any fellowship of the Spirit, if any bowels and mercies, 2 Fulfil ye my joy, that ye be likeminded, having the same love, being of one accord, of one mind.

Romans 15:5-7 — Now the God of patience and consolation grant you to be likeminded one toward another according to Christ Jesus: 6 That ye may with one mind and one mouth glorify God, even the Father of our Lord Jesus Christ. ⁷ Wherefore receive ye one another, as Christ also received us to the glory of God.

Philemon 1:7 — For we have great joy and consolation in thy love, because the bowels of the saints are refreshed by thee, brother.

Acts 20:1-2 — And after the uproar was ceased, Paul called unto him the disciples, and embraced them, and departed for to go into Macedonia. ² And when he had gone over those parts, and had given them much exhortation, he came into Greece,

Hebrews 10:24-25 — And let us consider one another to provoke unto love and to good works: ²⁵ Not forsaking the assembling of ourselves together, as the manner of some is; but exhorting one another: and so much the more, as ye see the day approaching.

Practical Application

- Encourage ourselves in the Lord.
- Stand on the promises of God.
- Cast down vain imaginations.
- Encourage others.
- Become an Encourager.
- Refuse to be discouraged, keep focused on the Lord.

Personal Experiences of Discouragement

My wife had a battle with cancer. It greatly discouraged us. She had the surgery and found out they needed to go in a second time. That's when we went to CTCA, (Cancer Treatment Center of

America). It was a place of encouragement in every manner, spiritually, physically, emotionally. A place of healing during this discouraging time. But God who by His grace and strength intervened, second surgery went flawless, follow up showed no traces of cancer. Five years later, she's still doing fine.

Conclusion

We all get discouraged at times. Pray for strength, suit up for battle, keep your confidence in the Lord, His promises and His word. I would like to share one last scripture:

Hebrews 10: 35-37 — Cast not away therefore your confidence, which hath great recompence of reward. 36 For ye have need of patience, that, after ye have done the will of God, ye might receive the promise. 37 For yet a little while, and he that shall come will come, and will not tarry.

CHAPTER 19

Overcoming Stress God's Way

(PSALM 120:1)

Introduction

Stress seems to be the prevalent characteristic of our modern day. In a world where we have had great strides in technology, advancement in medicines, and huge investments in physical exercise and nutrition we find so many complaining of being stressed. Let me ask you a question, how do you see yourself in stressful circumstances, as a victim or victor? Remember, we have the greater One, Jesus living inside of us. His spirit has been imparted into our very being at salvation. In this lesson we will look at God's way of handling the stresses of life.

Definition of Stress

Stress is defined as "Hardship, adversity, force, pressure," in part a shortening of Middle English distress ; in part from Old French estrece "narrowness, oppression," from Vulgar Latin *strictia, from Latin strictus means "tight, compressed, drawn together," past participle of stringere "draw tight". Meaning "physical strain on a material object"

Information on Stress

According to the most recent study, published by SingleCare last year, "more than three-quarters of adults report symptoms of stress, including headache, tiredness, and depression. Nearly half of all U.S. adults (49%) say that stress has negatively affected their behavior.

In 2023, the top causes of day-to-day stress in America were health (65%), money (63%), and the economy (64%), with other stressors including family responsibilities, personal safety, and discrimination."[1]

Glen Ryswyk, an Assemblies of God chaplain and clinical director of the Christian Family Counseling Center in Lawton, Okla., says *"stress is a symptom of a modern culture obsessed with performance and perfection."*

"We live in a world that is constantly pushing us to reach for more, find something better, work harder," Ryswyk says. *"Even in Christian circles, we buy into the idea that we have to keep demanding more of ourselves and everyone around us. We turn the crank tighter rather than depending on God's grace."*

Scriptures for Overcoming Stress and Worry

Matthew 11:28-30 Come unto me, all ye that labour and are heavy laden, and I will give you rest. [29] Take my yoke upon you,

---

[1] https://www.singlecare.com/blog/news/stress-statistics/

and learn of me; for I am meek and lowly in heart: and ye shall find rest unto your souls. [30] For my yoke is easy, and my burden is light.

I don't know of any more effective technique to get a handle on the stress in my life than to turn to Jesus. God designed you and me in a way that our spirit, mind and body would react together in a marvelous way when we feel tense and anxious and "heavy" and set our heart and mind on Jesus. God knew that Jesus was our anecdote for stress ... not drugs, food, alcohol and the internet. That's why he inspired Matthew to capture and write about Jesus' short teaching on this topic.

How do we "Come to Jesus?" We pray. We listen to inspirational music. We sit or walk quietly and listen for His voice. We cry out to Him in desperation. We read His Word, the Bible. We get on our knees and pour out our heart to Him. When we do this, He promises that He will give us

Psalm 9:9 The Lord also will be a refuge for the oppressed, a refuge in times of trouble.

Psalm 16:8 I have set the Lord always before me: because he is at my right hand, I shall not be moved.

Psalm 34:17-19 The righteous cry, and the LORD heareth, and delivereth them out of all their troubles. [18] The LORD is nigh unto them that are of a broken heart; and saveth such as be of a contrite spirit. [19] Many are the afflictions of the righteous: but the LORD delivereth him out of them all.

Psalm 46:1 God is our refuge and strength, a very present help in trouble.

Psalm 55:22 Cast thy burden upon the Lord, and he shall sustain thee: he shall never suffer the righteous to be moved.

Psalm 61:2-3 From the end of the earth will I cry unto thee, when my heart is overwhelmed: lead me to the rock that is higher than I. ³ For thou hast been a shelter for me, and a strong tower from the enemy.

Psalm 94:19 In the multitude of my thoughts within me thy comforts delight my soul.

Isaiah 40:30-31 Even the youths shall faint and be weary, and the young men shall utterly fall: ³¹ But they that wait upon the LORD shall renew their strength; they shall mount up with wings as eagles; they shall run, and not be weary; and they shall walk, and not faint.

Isaiah 41:10 Fear thou not; for I am with thee: be not dismayed; for I am thy God: I will strengthen thee; yea, I will help thee; yea, I will uphold thee with the right hand of my righteousness.

Matthew 6:25-27 Therefore I say unto you, Take no thought for your life, what ye shall eat, or what ye shall drink; nor yet for your body, what ye shall put on. Is not the life more than meat, and the body than raiment? ²⁶ Behold the fowls of the air: for they sow not, neither do they reap, nor gather into barns; yet your heavenly Father feedeth them. Are ye not much better than they? ²⁷ Which of you by taking thought can add one cubit unto his stature?

Matthew 6:34 Take therefore no thought for the morrow: for the morrow shall take thought for the things of itself. Sufficient unto the day is the evil thereof.

Matthew 11:28-30 ²⁸ Come unto me, all ye that labour and are heavy laden, and I will give you rest. ²⁹ Take my yoke upon you, and learn of me; for I am meek and lowly in heart: and ye shall find rest unto your souls. ³⁰ For my yoke is easy, and my burden is light.

Luke 10:41-42 And Jesus answered and said unto her, Martha, Martha, thou art careful and troubled about many things: ⁴² But one thing is needful: and Mary hath chosen that good part, which shall not be taken away from her.

John 14:1 Let not your heart be troubled: ye believe in God, believe also in me.

John 16:33 These things I have spoken unto you, that in me ye might have peace. In the world ye shall have tribulation: but be of good cheer; I have overcome the world.

Romans 8:28 And we know that all things work together for good to them that love God, to them who are the called according to his purpose.

Philippians 4:6-7 Be careful for nothing; but in every thing by prayer and supplication with thanksgiving let your requests be made known unto God. ⁷ And the peace of God, which passeth all understanding, shall keep your hearts and minds through Christ Jesus.

Philippians 4:19 But my God shall supply all your need according to his riches in glory by Christ Jesus.

Hebrews 13:6 So that we may boldly say, The Lord is my helper, and I will not fear what man shall do unto me.

James 1:2-4 My brethren, count it all joy when ye fall into divers temptations; ³ Knowing this, that the trying of your faith worketh patience. ⁴ But let patience have her perfect work, that ye may be perfect and entire, wanting nothing.

1 Peter 5:7 Casting all your care upon him; for he careth for you.

How God Uses Stress

When we see the all-powerful God on the throne of the universe — God our Father committed to our good — we are relieved of much stress. And the stress we must still experience leaves us far richer.

Having a biblical perspective is seeing life through God's eyes. It is seeing order in chaos, use in the useless, and good in the bad. If we are to develop eyes to see God's hand in everything, we must believe (not necessarily understand) what Scripture says about the purpose of stress. Stress is an effective tool in the hands of our God, a tool that is intended both for His glory and our good. In this article we will look at some ways God uses stress.

God uses stress to get our attention. God created our bodies. He designed them to send us messages. If I stick my hand in the fire, my body will send me a message, quickly and clearly. If I ignore it, I'll pay the price.

C.S. Lewis said *"pain is God's megaphone."* Some of us are hard of hearing. We ignore physical, mental, and spiritual warning signs. God wants us to tune our ears to the messages He sends us through our minds and bodies.

God uses stress to help us redefine or rediscover our priorities. Bill and Evelyn's marriage relationship was a distant one. They had drifted apart over many years, pouring themselves into their jobs and shortchanging their family. But when their son Jason was found in possession of heroin, the months that followed brought an unprecedented crisis… and the desire to pull their marriage back together.

Everyone has priorities. Some have never chosen or experienced the right ones and need to redefine them. Others of us have long known the right priorities and merely need to rediscover them: we've tasted right priorities, but we've allowed ourselves to drift away from them; we've replaced fellowship with entertainment, giving with buying, and family time with the television, the lawn, the remodeling job, the causes, and the committees.

By abandoning our God-given priorities, we set ourselves up to learn a hard lesson. In essence we do what the Israelites did: lived in paneled houses while God's house became a ruin (Haggai 1:4). In response, God sent lack of fulfillment, disillusionment, and failure as His messengers. He withheld His blessing till His people rediscovered their priorities.

Twice in Haggai 1:5-11, God's people are admonished to "Give careful thought to your ways." Stress should take us back to the basics. It is an opportunity to re-evaluate our priorities and bring them in line with God's.

God uses stress to draw us to Himself. Time and again it was said of the people of Israel, "But when they in their trouble did turn unto the Lord God of Israel, and sought him, he was found of them." (2 Chronicles 15:4). It was in Jonah's darkest hour, in his most stressful circumstances that he said this: "And said, I cried by reason of mine affliction unto the Lord, and he heard me; out of the belly of hell cried I, and thou heardest my voice." (Jonah 2:2). The Psalms are full of references of turning to God, seeking Him and finding Him in times of intense stress. Daniel in the lion's den sought God and He sent an angel to shut the lion's mouth (Daniel 6:22). Jesus in the Garden of Gethsemane in great distress prayed to His heavenly Father, not my will but thine be done (Matthew 26:39)

In my distress I called upon the Lord, and cried unto my God: he heard my voice out of his temple, and my cry came before him, even into his ears. (Psalm 18:6).

In my distress I cried unto the Lord, and he heard me. (Psalm 120:1).

When our lives are comfortable and stress-free, too often we withdraw from the Lord into our own worlds of spiritual independence and isolation. Smug and self-satisfied, we forget what life is really all about. But as the thirsty seek for water, those under stress often seek God. Many non-believers have come to Christ and many believers have returned to Him in times of stress.

God uses stress to discipline us. Quoting Solomon's words to his son, the writer of Hebrews offers what he calls a word of encouragement:

"My son, despise not thou the chastening of the Lord, nor faint when thou art rebuked of him: 6 For whom the Lord loveth he chasteneth, and scourgeth every son whom he receiveth. 7 If ye endure chastening, God dealeth with you as with sons; for what son is he whom the father chasteneth not?" Endure hardship as discipline; God is treating you as sons (Hebrews 12:5-7).

(The word son, of course, is generic for "child," and applies equally to God's daughters.)

To some of us, this doesn't sound so encouraging. But we fail to realize how essential discipline is. Scripture says that to withhold discipline from a child is, in essence, child abuse: "He that spareth his rod hateth his son: but he that loveth him chasteneth him betimes." (Proverbs 13:24). Discipline is corrective. It is remedial, not revengeful. God sends stresses not to get back at us for doing wrong, but to deepen our dependence on Him to do right. Though the stressful experience may seem excruciating at the time, it is ultimately all for good:

God disciplines us for our good that we may share in his holiness. No discipline seems pleasant at the time, but painful. Later, however, it produces a harvest of righteousness and peace for those who have been trained by it (Hebrews 12:10-11).

There is only one way a muscle grows — through stress. A muscle that is rarely exercised atrophies; it shrinks into uselessness. A muscle seldom stretched beyond its usual limits can only maintain itself. It cannot grow. To grow, a muscle must be taxed. Unusual demands must be placed upon it.

Ever seen grass grow through asphalt? It's amazing if you think about it. How does grass, pressed flat and robbed of light, persevere and break through hard ground? Yet we've seen it. Somehow God made those tiny blades of grass to rise to the greatest challenge.

In the crucible of stress, as we draw on our resources in Christ, He gives us faith and strength to crack through and rise above the asphalt coat of life under the curse and overcome the challenges of life.

Conclusion

Stress is a demand placed upon our faith. Without it our faith will not, cannot, grow. God uses stress to strengthen our faith. 1 Peter 1:7 tells us: "That the trial of your faith, being much more precious than of gold that perisheth, though it be tried with fire, might be found unto praise and honour and glory at the appearing of Jesus Christ:"

CHAPTER 20

The Power Of Patience (Perseverance)

(HEBREWS 12:1-2)

Introduction

The development of patience is an important part of our becoming like Christ (see 2 Peter 1:5–8). Being patient … for healing, for deliverance, for guidance, for training … is often difficult. The ability to endure and continue despite hardship is a virtue that reaps great rewards. We want things to happen now, not somewhere in the distant future.

Time never drags more slowly than when we are waiting for someone to arrive, or for something to take place. But the best things seem to require a great deal of patience. A doctor must study for seven to ten years before he can realize his goal. A parent must teach his child the same lesson repeatedly before it is learned. Most of us work hard and save our money for a long period of time before we can have something that is important to us.

And the Spirit filled Christian must learn the secret of patience if a Christ like character is to be developed in them. People often speak of the patience of Job. Job suffered long and waited patiently upon the Lord before he received healing and the restoration of his family and possessions. Moses spent 40 years in the school of patience before he reached his potential in usefulness for the Lord in leading over a million Israelites out of Egyptian bondage. We are advised to "Be ye also patient; stablish your hearts: for the coming of the Lord draweth nigh." (James 5:8).

Greek and Hebrew Definition

Greek Definition of Perseverance

The greek word is hypomonế (from 5259 /hypō, "under" and 3306 /ménō, "remain, endure") — remaining under, endurance; steadfastness, especially as God enables the believer to "remain (endure) under" the challenges He allows in life.

Hebrew Definition of Perseverance

The Hebrew word is sarah: to persist, exert oneself, persevere

Expanded Definition of (Patience) Perseverance

The definition of perseverance means that they have a determined continuation in something with a steady and continued action of belief that occurs over a long period of time amongst and despite especially difficult circumstances. That seems to fit nicely with the biblical definition of the patience of the saints of God who after being saved must endure many trials, tests, tribulations and persecution from non-believers and others. They continue steadfast in their faith because their faith is not their own but in God and it is not the strength of their faith that allows them to endure but their faith is only as strong as the Object of their faith and that is Jesus Christ.

Based on a true story, Track coach Jim White (Kevin Costner) is a newcomer to a predominantly Latino high school in California's Central Valley. Coach White and his new students find that they have much to learn about one another, but things begin to change when White realizes the boys' exceptional running ability. What he also admires, is before they arrive at school, they would have to get up at 4 am in the morning, work in the fields and then go to school because the parents and family need them to work the fields to bring in needed income for survival.

He cannot train them during school hours. He then decides to train them after school and work around their schedules. More than just physical prowess drives the teens to succeed; their strong family ties, incredible work ethic and commitment to their team and a faith in God all play a factor in forging these novice runners into champions.

From 1980 to 2003, his team won nine state championships in Divisions III and IV, as well as numerous lesser titles. It is a true story of how even during difficult circumstances and hardship can we develop perseverance and endurance and overcome life's challenges. What we sometimes want to run from, God uses to fulfill His purposes in our lives and the lives of others.

Steadfastness Produces Perseverance

James 1:2-4, 12 ESV. "Count it all joy, my brothers, when you meet trials of various kinds, 2 for you know that the testing of your faith produces steadfastness. ³ And let steadfastness have its full effect, ⁴ that you may be perfect and complete, lacking in nothing.

¹² Blessed is the man who remains steadfast (or perseveres) under trial, for when he has stood the test he will receive the crown of life, which God has promised to those who love him."

There is a lot here. We not only will have to endure "trials of various kinds", but we must "count it all joy." The one who perseveres knows that "the testing of [their] faith produces steadfastness." When this "steadfastness [has] its full effect...you may be perfect and complete, lacking in nothing." None of us are perfect so when we examine the Greek word for "perfect" which is "teleios" we see that it means that our faith is "brought to its end" or "finished" which is what the word complete means in Greek "holokleros" or "complete in all parts" or "whole." Just as metal is tested by fire and becomes stronger, so too is our faith tested and made stronger. Those who stand "the test...will receive the *crown of life*, which God has promised to those who love him." *James 1:12*

Suffering Produces Perseverance

Romans 5:3-4 ESV "We rejoice in our sufferings, knowing that suffering produces endurance, ⁴ and endurance produces character, and character produces hope."

We must admit that we have our weak moments and feel that we cannot go on, so it is very difficult to imagine how we are supposed to "rejoice in our sufferings." We can rejoice in them if we know that we are secure in the Lord (**John 10:28-29**) and with the knowledge that our "suffering produces endurance." When I was on the track team in high school, there was suffering during training when I got what the trainer called "shin splints." These are tiny hairline fractures in the bones and they were very painful, but the continual running eventually built up the bones and I could endure the suffering because it produced a longer, stronger endurance in me.

This endurance produced character in me to not give up and this endurance that my character had developed through the sufferings gave me hope. It gave me hope that I could endure the mile run and finish because I didn't give up. My suffering produced my endurance, my endurance produced character, and this character created hope in my ability to finish the race. The same goes with the Christian who suffers. One follows the other by necessity. If we suffer with Him, we shall also reign with Him. *2 Tim 2:12a*

Endurance Produces Perseverance

Hebrews 12:1-2 ESV "Therefore, since we are surrounded by so great a cloud of witnesses, let us also lay aside every weight, and sin which clings so closely, and let us run with endurance the race that is set before us, [2] looking to Jesus, the founder and perfecter of our faith, who for the joy that was set before him endured the cross, despising the shame, and is seated at the right hand of the throne of God."

Anytime the word "therefore" is at the beginning of a sentence, we must ask what is the therefore, there for? In this case, the "therefore" is there because of what preceded it in Hebrews chapter

11 which is what we call "The Hall of Faith." This chapter is full of the testimonies of the Old Testament saints who had to endure severe trials but they were still able to complete the race and make it across the finish line.

The author of Hebrews portrays our race to the finish line (the kingdom) like a runner in stadiums that are full of previous winners, the saints of the Old Testament, who are cheering us on. In our running, we must imagine seeing the finish line and the cloud of witnesses and see Jesus who is presently "seated at the right hand of the throne of God" waiting for us. To run a race we must take off every unnecessary weight (things of the world) and every "sin which clings so closely" to us that unless we rid ourselves of these we will be slowed down considerably and the race will take much longer.

Suffering Produces Perseverance

Second Thessalonians 1:4-5 ESV "Therefore we ourselves boast about you in the churches of God for your steadfastness and faith in all your persecutions and in the afflictions that you are enduring. [5] This is evidence of the righteous judgment of God, that you may be considered worthy of the kingdom of God, for which you are also suffering."

Paul was so proud of the church at Thessalonica that he bragged about them to the other churches. Why? It was because of their steadfast faith under severe persecutions and afflictions. Since they were enduring, Paul called this the "evidence of the righteous judgment of God." How is this evidence of the "righteous judgment of God?" It is evidence that they are saved, and a saved person endures till the end, and this is proof that they "may be considered worthy of the kingdom for which [they were] suffering" for.

Exposing False Teachers Produces Perseverance

Revelation 2:2-3 ESV, "I know your works, your toil and your patient endurance, and how you cannot bear with those who are evil, but have tested those who call themselves apostles and are not, and found them to be false. ³ I know you are enduring patiently and bearing up for my name's sake, and you have not grown weary."

Jesus addresses the church or church age of Ephesus. Jesus knows their works, their toil, and their patient endurance since He is the Head of the Church and knows everything about what the church goes through. Jesus seems to boast about their inability to "bear with those who are evil" by testing "those who call themselves apostles and are not and found them to be false." That is a high compliment because this is a church that doesn't water down the truth.

Those "who call themselves apostles are [most certainly] not" because in all the New Testament it was Jesus Who called the apostles. Not once did a person ever call themselves to be an apostle. They had to have been with Jesus from the beginning up to the time of His resurrection and had to be an eyewitness of it. When they had to find a replacement for Judas Iscariot, they understood that the qualifications were that "one of the men who have accompanied us during all the time that the Lord Jesus went in and out among us, [22] beginning from the baptism of John until the day when he was taken up from us — one of these men must become with us a witness to his resurrection." (Acts 1:21-22 ESV).

The point is that if someone today calls themselves an apostle, they could not possibly be qualified to be one and Luke, the author of Acts, knows this as did the other apostles and so apparently did the church at Ephesus. That is because "they devoted themselves to the apostles' teaching and the fellowship, to the breaking of bread and the prayers." (Acts 2:42 ESV) and the apostles were those who had been with Christ, not those who proclaimed themselves as ones.

Personal Testimony of Perseverance

I remember running track in high school. I did not like running but I wanted to be part of a team. I did not make the football team or the basketball team, but I did make the track team. I was too slow to be a sprinter, so I was trained to run the mile. It was a grueling workout. I despised it yet my friends were there as part of the team and I endured it for the team. You would run a mile at full speed and instead of resting the coach would have us line up again and run another one. And then another one.

Once I ran so much that my arches were in great pain and could not run anymore. Yet with warm water and massage therapy I was able to run again this time stronger and faster. At our first track meet I looked at these big guys and said they are going to beat us. As it turned out, because of the hard training we beat all the runners. Had I quit at the first sign of pain I would have never discovered my potential and the great miler I had become (at least in my opinion).

Conclusion

The Christian life is compared to a race. In Hebrews 12:1-2 "Therefore, since we are surrounded by so great a cloud of witnesses, let us also lay aside every weight, and sin which clings so closely, and let us run with endurance the race that is set before us, [2] looking to Jesus, the founder and perfecter of our faith, who for the joy that was set before him endured the cross, despising the shame, and is seated at the right hand of the throne of God." Let's run this race with the understanding the crowd in heaven is watching us, laying aside sin, and run this race with patience (perseverance) looking to Jesus our savior and with a joy in our heart knowing that one day we will receive the reward of heaven and its manifold blessings.

CHAPTER 21

Prayer And Fasting

(MATTHEW 17:20-21)

Introduction

Prayer is a powerful force in this world. It is a communion between man and God. It's a communion that can hold back the forces of the enemy, bring healing, provision, meet the deepest needs of our life, save the lost. Yet when we pray and fast there is an anointing, strengthening of the spirit man in us, that can bring deliverance from bondages and demonic strongholds in our lives and in the lives of others.

Scriptures on Prayer and Fasting

Fasting To Be Seen

Luke 18:11-12 — "The Pharisee stood and prayed thus with himself, God, I thank thee, that I am not as other men are, extortioners, unjust, adulterers, or even as this publican. [12] I fast twice in the week, I give tithes of all that I possess."

Here is an open, public display of someone wanting to appear righteous in front of others (self-righteous) and to boast that they fast "twice a week" and give tithes and are not like adulterers, tax collectors, or extortioners. He is right...he is not like them...he is worse! God resists the proud (James 4:6).

This Pharisee fasted for all the wrong reasons. He did it to be seen by men, he did it to proclaim that he is righteous when he is self-righteous and, in his arrogance, he boasts that he is not like sinners. He doesn't get it. That is legalism. For him to fast for these reasons is to be legalistic. He has already received his reward by being seen. This means that there will be no reward from God. His efforts are in vain. In fact, it would have been better for him to not fast at all because he was doing it for all the wrong reasons.

Fasting for God's Intervention

Second Samuel 12:15-17 "And Nathan departed unto his house. And the LORD struck the child that Uriah's wife bare unto David, and it was very sick. [16] David therefore besought God for the child; and David fasted, and went in, and lay all night upon the earth. [17] And the elders of his house arose, and went to him, to raise him up from the earth: but he would not, neither did he eat bread with them."

Here we see another reason to fast; David was petitioning or asking for God's intervention on behalf of his sick child. David fasted because he understood why the child had been afflicted. It was due to his sins of adultery and murder. We can fast when someone we love is sick, we can fast for revival for our church and for ourselves, we can fast for spiritual growth, we can fast to seek God's will in an important decision, we can fast for someone's salvation, deliverance, we can fast for overcoming an addiction (like in Isaiah 56:3-7), we can fast during times of great loss or grief over a loved one dying, we can fast for any number of reasons that are personal and for others.

Fasting Requires Humbling Ourselves Before God

Psalms 35:13-14 — David said, "But as for me, when they were sick, my clothing was sackcloth: I humbled my soul with fasting; and my prayer returned into mine own bosom. ¹⁴ I behaved myself as though he had been my friend or brother: I bowed down heavily, as one that mourneth for his mother."

There are fewer things that we can do to make us see our need for God than to fast. During times of fasting, we see just how much we depend upon God for our sustenance.

I cannot nor can you survive without God for very long because He gives us all good things to enjoy (1 Tim 6:17; James 1:17). David said it was good that he afflicted himself. Almost every time you read the word "afflicted" in the Bible, it speaks of fasting. The word David used for "afflict" is the Hebrew word "anah" and it means to "afflict, oppress, humble, and be bowed down" and this is exactly what fasting does...it humbles you. Maybe you have heard the saying that the word of God comforts the afflicted and afflicts the comfortable. This is so true but fewer things will humble us before our God than to fast.

Fasting to Resist Sin and Be Strengthened for Spiritual Warfare

Matthew 4: 1-11, Then was Jesus led up of the Spirit into the wilderness to be tempted of the devil. ² And when he had fasted forty days and forty nights, he was afterward an hungred. ³ And when the tempter came to him, he said, If thou be the Son of God, command that these stones be made bread. ⁴ But he answered and said, It is written, Man shall not live by bread alone, but by every word that proceedeth out of the mouth of God. ⁵ Then the devil taketh him up into the holy city, and setteth him on a pinnacle of the temple, ⁶ And saith unto him, If thou be the Son of God, cast thyself down: for it is written, He shall give his angels charge concerning thee: and in their hands they shall bear thee up, lest at any time thou dash thy foot against a stone. ⁷ Jesus said unto him, It is written again, Thou shalt not tempt the Lord thy God.

⁸ Again, the devil taketh him up into an exceeding high mountain, and sheweth him all the kingdoms of the world, and the glory of them; ⁹ And saith unto him, All these things will I give thee, if thou wilt fall down and worship me. ¹⁰ Then saith Jesus unto him, Get thee hence, Satan: for it is written, Thou shalt worship the Lord thy God, and him only shalt thou serve. ¹¹ Then the devil leaveth him, and, behold, angels came and ministered unto him.

We see in these verses and the ones following one of the greatest battles between Jesus and Satan. Each time satan tempted Jesus, He came back with the word of God, strong and anointed in the spirit. When we are facing spiritual battles, temptation and oppression from satan, fasting will strengthen us in our spirit, to fight and overcome our enemy the devil.

Some Kinds of Demonic Oppressions Come out Only By Prayer and Fasting

Matthew 17:14-21 — And when they were come to the multitude, there came to him a certain man, kneeling down to him, and saying, ¹⁵ Lord, have mercy on my son: for he is lunatick, and sore vexed: for ofttimes he falleth into the fire, and oft into the water. ¹⁶ And I brought him to thy disciples, and they could not cure him. ¹⁷ Then Jesus answered and said, O faithless and perverse generation, how long shall I be with you? how long shall I suffer you? bring him hither to me.

¹⁸ And Jesus rebuked the devil; and he departed out of him: and the child was cured from that very hour. ¹⁹ Then came the disciples to Jesus apart, and said, Why could not we cast him out? ²⁰ And Jesus said unto them, Because of your unbelief: for verily I say unto you, If ye have faith as a grain of mustard seed, ye shall say unto this mountain, Remove hence to yonder place; and it shall remove; and nothing shall be impossible unto you. ²¹ Howbeit this kind goeth not out but by prayer and fasting.

We see Jesus revealing to His disciples why they could not cast out this spirit from this young boy. The first reason He told them was because of their unbelief, why they doubted, we are not sure since they had been given authority over all the powers of the enemy by Jesus. One reason could be that the human side of them like Peter who walked on the waters started to sink because of unbelief as he looked at the waves and maybe they had their eyes on the situation which caused them to doubt. The second reason is

Jesus told them that this kind of demon can only come out by prayer and fasting. *We know that prayer and fasting is a strengthening of faith and causes a release of greater anointing of the Lord upon our lives, which, evidently, is what the disciples needed to cast this kind of demon out.*

Personal Testimony of Prayer and Fasting

During a time of prayer and fasting I saw God do different things. I saw my son have a change of heart and began to be more submissive and more peaceful and move in a better direction in his personal life. My wife and I experienced a closer presence of the Lord in our lives. I was healed of a terrible pain in my shoulder that just came upon me suddenly. Spiritual attacks would come but they did not last long as the Lord strengthened our spirits. New opportunities opened at work, and other personal answers to prayers. The Lord has proven Himself to be mighty in battle.

Conclusion

What battles are you facing today, what bondages are you battling, feeling discouraged and defeated, no answers to prayers, need your faith strengthened, are there strongholds in your family, with your friends, facing impossible situations? Pray and fast, for it was Jesus who said that some kinds of demonic attacks go out only by prayer and fasting. Let us join and unite and see the enemy defeated and the victory of the Lord be established.

CHAPTER 22

Returning To Our First Love

(MATTHEW 22:37)

Introduction

Every New Year people talk about new resolutions and changes they plan to make. Let me challenge you, if you will make loving God and Jesus fresh and new in your life again, it will be the greatest resolution for the New Year you will ever make. Let's begin, Jesus was asked the question by an expert in the law; what was the greatest commandment? Without hesitation Jesus states 'You shall love the Lord your God with all your heart, all your soul, and with all your mind. This is the first and great commandment.

I have some questions for you: Have you left your first love of Him, the One who loves you with an everlasting love? The One who loved you so much that He died and bled for you and paid a great price for you? The One whose love has forgiven and covered your sins by His blood? In this study we will see why it is so important that our love for Him should be the top priority and motivation in all our lives.

Reading of Biography of St Francis of Assisi

Born in London, G.K. Chesterton was educated at St. Paul's,

but never went to college. He went to art school. In 1900, he was asked to contribute a few magazine articles on art criticism and went on to become one of the most prolific writers of all time. He says this about St. Francis of Assisi born in the 12th century. St Francis did not love humanity but men, so he did not love Christianity but Christ. To this great man religion was not a thing like a theory but a thing like a love affair. It was reality to him.

Reading of Matthew 22:34-40 and Commentary

[34] But when the Pharisees had heard that he had put the Sadducees to silence, they were gathered together. [35] Then one of them, which was a lawyer, asked him a question, tempting him, and saying, [36] Master, which is the great commandment in the law? [37] Jesus said unto him, THOU SHALT LOVE THE LORD THY GOD WITH ALL THY HEART, AND WITH ALL THY SOUL, AND WITH ALL THY MIND. [38] This is the first and great commandment. [39] And the second is like unto it, THOU SHALT LOVE THY NEIGHBOUR AS THYSELF. [40] On these two commandments hang all the law and the prophets.

Benson Commentary

When the Pharisees heard that he had put the Sadducees to silence —
Gr. οτι εφιμοσε, that he had stopped their mouths, or so confuted that he
had confounded them, and rendered them unable to make any reply; they
were gathered together — It is not said with what design: but it is

probable from Matthew 22:15-16, with a malicious one, namely, to try, though the Sadducees had been baffled in their attempt upon him, as they themselves had also been, when they united with the Herodians, if they could yet any way expose him to the people. Then one of them, a lawyer — Or teacher of the law, (namely, of Moses,) as the word νομικος *always means in the New Testament, that is, a scribe, asked him a question, tempting, or trying him — Not, it seems, with any ill design, but barely to make further trial of that wisdom which he had shown in silencing the Sadducees.*

For, according to Mark, it was in consequence of his perceiving that our Lord had answered the Sadducees well, that this person asked the question here mentioned. Master, which is the great commandment in the law? — This was a famous question among the Jews. "Some of their doctors declared that the law of sacrifices was the great commandment, because sacrifices were both the expiations or forgiveness of sin and thanksgivings for mercies; others bestowed this honor on the law of circumcision, because it was the sign of the covenant established between God and the nation; a third sort yielded to the law of the Sabbath, because, by that appointment, both the knowledge and practice of the institutions of Moses were preserved; and to name no more, there were some who affirmed the law of meats and washings to be of the greatest importance, because thereby the people of God were effectually separated from the company and conversations of the heathen." But Jesus, with much better reason, decided in favor of a command inclusive of the whole of piety, and leading to every holy temper, word, and work. That command was to Love God and others by deeds and actions not merely words

Matthew Henry's Concise Commentary

An interpreter of the law asked our Lord a question, to try, not so much his knowledge, as his judgment. The love of God is the first and great commandment, and the sum of all the commands of the first tablet. Our love of God must be sincere, not in word and tongue only. All our love is too little to bestow upon him, therefore all the powers of the soul must be engaged for him and carried out toward him. To love our neighbor as ourselves, is the second great commandment. There is a self-love which is corrupt, and the root of the greatest sins and it must be put off and mortified; but there is a self-love which is the rule of the greatest duty: we must have a due concern for the welfare of our own souls and bodies. And we must love our neighbor as truly and sincerely as we love ourselves; in many cases we must deny ourselves for the good of others. By these two commandments let our hearts be formed as by a mold.

Verse by Verse Study of the Scriptures of Matthew 22:34-40

The Pharisees came together against Jesus; they could not defeat Him one on one with their arguments, so they gathered. One of them, a lawyer probably was the most knowledgeable of the group, takes the challenge and asks Him a question testing His knowledge. Little did he and the others realize that the son of the God of the universe, of the all-knowing God was in their midst. There was no question He could not answer.

They ask Jesus what the greatest commandment in the law was referring to the Law of Moses. Again, they did not realize that He was before Moses and was there when Moses was given the Ten commandments.

With full authority and confidence Jesus answers the lawyer's question that YOU SHALL LOVE THE LORD YOUR GOD WITH ALL YOUR HEART, AND WITH ALL YOUR SOUL, AND WITH ALL YOUR MIND. Jesus starts off by stating that love should be our motivation. He then refers to God as your God, in other words God is the creator of all mankind. Notice Jesus uses the word <u>All</u>. God is worthy of *all* our life. We should glorify Him in our heart, with our life and our thinking.

When we love Him with our *all,* He is above *all* other relationships and things. We will then love others properly and love people more than the things of this world. Jesus again states that this is the greatest commandment of all. It is when we love God that we will keep His commandments and live holy and obedient lives. Then He said the second commandment was to love others as ourselves. When we love others as ourselves, we will not lie to them, cheat them, we will treat them with respect, forgive them and do good to them. God is a relational God, and relationships are important to Him and others.

Then Jesus ends this discourse on love by stating, on these two commandments hang all the law and the prophets. In the entire Bible we see God reaching out to man to redeem him, to restore him, rescue him and deliver him from the evil one and the evils of this world. Why does God pursue mankind, it is because He loves them. He also desires that His people live in love, unity and peace with one another and holiness without which no man will see the Lord.

Practical Ways of Returning to Our First Love

(Revelation 2:3-5) And hast borne, and hast patience, and for my name's sake hast laboured, and hast not fainted. ⁴Nevertheless I have somewhat against thee, because thou hast left thy first love. ⁵Remember therefore from whence thou art fallen, and repent, and do the first works; or else I will come unto thee quickly, and will remove thy candlestick out of his place, except thou repent.

Things to Consider

- Let's remember when we were first saved and in love with Jesus, we seem to love everybody, even our enemies.
- Remember the closeness we had with Him, the answer to prayers, His mercy that He showered upon us, He is still the same Lord.
- Let's go back and do our first works again, praying, spending time with Him, watching Christian TV, listening to Christian music and telling others about Him.
- When we do feel our hearts getting cold, let's be quick to repent and turn toward Him, the lover of our soul.
- Let's do our part and guard our affection and love for Him and not allow offenses, anger, bitterness, or unforgiveness stand between us and His love for us.
- Let's go back and read the love chapter in 1st Corinthians 13, and practice those virtues of kindness, patience, and humility.
- If we feel far from Him, remember He has not moved, we

have moved. The scripture states draw near to God and He will draw near to us (James 4:8).

Personal Experiences

It was the love of God shown through others that eventually won my heart. I remember the story about a woman who was an atheist. Yet on her job she felt drawn to two women who were Christians because of the peace and love she felt while being around them. They didn't preach to her. Yet one of them began to invite her to church and would not let up. So, one day she said she would go, if the lady would stop inviting her.

She went and sat way in the back. She said that as the singing began, she could literally feel the love of God touching her by His spirit and she began to weep. When the altar call was given, she readily accepted the Lord and now appears on TBN sharing her testimony how she was won by the love she felt by the spirit of God and in one moment of time was miraculously converted from a life of atheism. Many are won to Jesus by believers allowing His love and compassion to flow through them.

Conclusion

As believers we need to ask ourselves, do we love the stories about Jesus or Jesus? Do we love ministry or the Lord of the ministry? Have we left our first love and settled for a Christian life of just going through the motions and appearances, but our hearts are not into it? That all can be changed if we just return to our first love, Jesus.

CHAPTER 23

Trusting In The Lord

When Life Circumstances are Confusing

Introduction

It is easy to trust, to confide, believe and have a positive attitude when life is going well, according to plan, it makes sense. Yet there are times in life when nothing in our life circumstances can be explained, it can get confusing. Those are the times we need to trust in the Lord and not lean to our own understanding. Today we will be studying the Book of Job and how a man who endured such adversity and confusing circumstances and yet never lost his faith and trust in God.

Background and Overview on the Book of Job

The author of the book of Job is unknown. Several suggestions have been put forth as plausible authors: Job himself, who could have best recalled his own words; Elihu, the fourth friend who spoke toward the end of the story; various biblical writers and leaders; or many editors who compiled the material over the years. While there is no definite answer, it was most likely an eyewitness who recorded the detailed and lengthy conversations found in the book. In Old Testament times, authors sometimes referred to themselves in the third person, so Job's authorship is a strong possibility. Who was Job? This wealthy landowner and father is one of the best-known biblical heroes. But we know little more than that he was stripped of everything, without warning, and that his faith was severely tested.

The book delves into issues near to the heart of every human who experiences suffering. The prologue provides a fascinating peek into the back story — why God allowed Satan to afflict Job with such pain and turmoil. Then, through a series of dialogues and monologues arranged in a pattern of threes, human wisdom attempts to explain the unexplainable, until finally God Himself speaks. The final chapters of Job record God's masterful defense of His majesty and unique "otherness" — of God's eternal transcendence above creation — in contrast with Job's humble and ignorant mortality. "Where were you when I laid the foundation of the earth? Tell Me, if you can.

Pain inevitably afflicts each one of us. Suffering is unavoidable in this life.

Attack on His Possessions

Job 1:9-22 Then Satan answered the LORD, and said, Doth Job fear God for nought? [10] Hast not thou made an hedge about him, and about his house, and about all that he hath on every side? thou hast blessed the work of his hands, and his substance is increased in the land. ¹¹ But put forth thine hand now, and touch all that he hath, and he will curse thee to thy face. ¹² And the LORD said unto Satan, Behold, all that he hath is in thy power; only upon himself put not forth thine hand. So Satan went forth from the presence of the LORD.

Satan Allowed to Test Job

¹³ And there was a day when his sons and his daughters were eating and drinking wine in their eldest brother's house:

¹⁴ And there came a messenger unto Job, and said, The oxen were plowing, and the asses feeding beside them: ¹⁵ And the Sabeans fell upon them, and took them away; yea, they have slain the servants with the edge of the sword; and I only am escaped alone to tell thee. ¹⁶ While he was yet speaking, there came also another, and said, The fire of God is fallen from heaven, and hath burned up the sheep, and the servants, and consumed them; and I only am escaped alone to tell thee.

¹⁷ While he was yet speaking, there came also another, and said, The Chaldeans made out three bands, and fell upon the camels, and have carried them away, yea, and slain the servants with the edge of the sword; and I only am escaped alone to tell thee. ¹⁸ While he was yet speaking, there came also another, and said, Thy sons and thy daughters were eating and drinking wine in their eldest brother's house: ¹⁹ And, behold, there came a great wind from the wilderness, and smote the four corners of the house, and it fell upon the young men, and they are dead; and I only am escaped alone to tell thee.

²⁰ Then Job arose, and rent his mantle, and shaved his head, and fell down upon the ground, and worshipped,

²¹ And said, Naked came I out of my mother's womb, and naked shall I return thither: the LORD gave, and the LORD hath taken away; blessed be the name of the LORD. ²² In all this Job sinned not, nor charged God foolishly.

Attack on His Physical Person

Again there was a day when the sons of God came to present themselves before the LORD, and Satan came also among them to present himself before the LORD. ² And the LORD said unto Satan, From whence comest thou? And Satan answered the LORD, and said, From going to and fro in the earth, and from walking up and down in it. ³ And the LORD said unto Satan, Hast thou considered my servant Job, that there is none like him in the earth, a perfect and an upright man, one that feareth God, and escheweth evil? and still he holdeth fast his integrity, although thou movedst me against him, to destroy him without cause.

⁴ And Satan answered the LORD, and said, Skin for skin, yea, all that a man hath will he give for his life. ⁵ But put forth thine hand now, and touch his bone and his flesh, and he will curse thee to thy face. ⁶ And the LORD said unto Satan, Behold, he is in thine hand; but save his life. ⁷ So went Satan forth from the presence of the LORD, and smote Job with sore boils from the sole of his foot unto his crown. ⁸ And he took him a potsherd to scrape himself withal; and he sat down among the ashes. ⁹ Then said his wife unto him, Dost thou still retain thine integrity? curse God, and die. ¹⁰ But

he said unto her, Thou speakest as one of the foolish women speaketh. What? shall we receive good at the hand of God, and shall we not receive evil? In all this did not Job sin with his lips.

Job Curses the Day He was Born

Job 3: 1–7 After this opened Job his mouth, and cursed his day. ² And Job spake, and said,

³ Let the day perish wherein I was born, and the night in which it was said, There is a man child conceived. ⁴ Let that day be darkness; let not God regard it from above, neither let the light shine upon it. ⁵ Let darkness and the shadow of death stain it; let a cloud dwell upon it; let the blackness of the day terrify it. ⁶ As for that night, let darkness seize upon it; let it not be joined unto the days of the year, let it not come into the number of the months. ⁷ Lo, let that night be solitary, let no joyful voice come therein.

God Speaks to Job

(During this dialogue God asks Job over 184 questions.)

Job 38:1-13 Then the LORD answered Job out of the whirlwind, and said, ² Who is this that darkeneth counsel by words without knowledge? ³ Gird up now thy loins like a man; for I will demand of thee, and answer thou me. ⁴ Where wast thou when I laid the foundations of the earth? declare, if thou hast understanding.

⁵ Who hath laid the measures thereof, if thou knowest? or who hath stretched the line upon it? ⁶ Whereupon are the foundations thereof fastened? or who laid the corner stone thereof; ⁷ When the

morning stars sang together, and all the sons of God shouted for joy? [8] Or who shut up the sea with doors, when it brake forth, as if it had issued out of the womb? [9] When I made the cloud the garment thereof, and thick darkness a swaddlingband for it, [10] And brake up for it my decreed place, and set bars and doors, [11] And said, Hitherto shalt thou come, but no further: and here shall thy proud waves be stayed? [12] Hast thou commanded the morning since thy days; and caused the dayspring to know his place; [13] That it might take hold of the ends of the earth, that the wicked might be shaken out of it?

God Displeased with Job's Friends

Job 42: 7-9. And it was so, that after the LORD had spoken these words unto Job, the LORD said to Eliphaz the Temanite, My wrath is kindled against thee, and against thy two friends: for ye have not spoken of me the thing that is right, as my servant Job hath. [8] Therefore take unto you now seven bullocks and seven rams, and go to my servant Job, and offer up for yourselves a burnt offering; and my servant Job shall pray for you: for him will I accept: lest I deal with you after your folly, in that ye have not spoken of me the thing which is right, like my servant Job. [9] So Eliphaz the Temanite and Bildad the Shuhite and Zophar the Naamathite went, and did according as the LORD commanded them: the LORD also accepted Job.

The Latter End of Job Where God Blesses Him for His Trust

Job 42: 10-17. And the LORD turned the captivity of Job, when he prayed for his friends: also the LORD gave Job twice as much as he had before. [11] Then came there unto him all his brethren, and all his sisters, and all they that had been of his acquaintance before, and did eat bread with him in his house: and they bemoaned him, and comforted him over all the evil that the LORD had brought upon him: every man also gave him a piece of money, and every one an earring of gold. [12] So the LORD blessed the latter end of Job more than his beginning: for he had fourteen thousand sheep, and six thousand camels, and a thousand yoke of oxen, and a thousand she asses. [13] He had also seven sons and three daughters. [14] And he called the name of the first, Jemima; and the name of the second, Kezia; and the name of the third, Kerenhappuch. [15] And in all the land were no women found so fair as the daughters of Job: and their father gave them inheritance among their brethren. [16] After this lived Job an hundred and forty years, and saw his sons, and his sons' sons, even four generations. [17] So Job died, being old and full of days.

Conclusion

Will your relationship with God be enough when trials come? Will you trust Him through your suffering? Spend time with the Almighty. Pray for a stronger faith in the powerful Creator described in those chapters. Pray for a right perspective of Him so that you might see your situation through His eyes. Instead of asking where God is during your pain, the book of Job affirms God's control and asks us, "Where are we in our pain? Are we trusting our Creator, even though we cannot understand our circumstances? And to be assured that God will show His mercy and lovingkindness to us as He did to Job for our trust in Him.

CHAPTER 24

Vain Imaginations

(2 CORINTHIANS 10:15)

Introduction

There is a difference between imagination and vain imaginations. The bible speaks about casting down vain worthless imaginations. Satan is a master mind of trying to encourage us to think upon vain imaginations or thoughts. We are not to dwell upon them, for they can become strongholds, but to take spiritual authority over them and cast them down in the name of Jesus and move forward in faith to the work He has for us.

Definition of Imaginations

Greek word is phantasia — show, display Bible dictionary — "a shaping," hence, "a thought" reasoning through. Websters definition — the act or power of forming a mental image of something not present to the senses or never before wholly perceived in reality.

Greek word for Vain — mátín (an adverb) — properly, "aimlessly"; pointless, without ground or any real purpose.

Webster's definition — The definition of vain is someone or

something without value, ... in vain. Fruitlessly, vainly; lightly; profanely; irreverently

So, in short, vain imaginations are imaginations that are worthless, without any truth in them.

Key Verse

2nd Corinthians 10:5 Casting down imaginations, and every high thing that exalteth itself against the knowledge of God and bringing into captivity every thought to the obedience of Christ.

Reading in Context

[3] For though we walk in the flesh, we do not war after the flesh: [4] For the weapons of our warfare are not carnal, but mighty through God to the pulling down of strong holds; [5] Casting down imaginations and every high thing that exalteth itself against the knowledge of God and bringing into captivity every thought to the obedience of Christ.

How To Cast Down Vain Imaginations

Paul wrote that we do not war according to the flesh (2 Cor. 10:3-5). Our warfare is not of this world; it is divinely powerful for the destruction of fortresses. That is, if you have a stronghold, which is a deeply embedded sinful habit pattern, you can pull it down and destroy it by appropriating the powerful spiritual warfare that is ours in Christ.

We destroy "vain imaginations" (KJV), speculations and every lofty thing raised up against the knowledge of God, by casting down any thought that does not line up with the Word of God or what we know of the Son of God. We take the thought captive to the obedience of Christ. That is, we march the thought that we captured before we acted upon it and present our captive thought to our Commander in Chief, Jesus Christ. We believe in Him to crucify the thought and by faith thank Him for doing so. Then we continue our walk of faith. Great truth. Now how does it work?

Thought — "I am such a bad Christian that God could never really love me."

Truth — that thought does not line up with the Word of God. 1st John 4:10 says, "Herein is love, not that we loved God, but that he loved us, and sent his Son to be the propitiation for our sins." (See, this is why you must know the Word of God! How else will you recognize the vain imaginations that are lifted up against the knowledge of God?) Here is a test for you — Do put-downs come easily?

Has your self-worth been so debased that you really believe the lies the enemy is shooting your way? Can you capture the thought before you act upon it (giving into depression or self-loathing) and turn to the Lord, marching the thought at gunpoint (mentally) to your Commander in Chief and asking Him to crucify the thought achieving victory through Christ? You have taken your thought captive to the obedience of Christ, cast down the lies of the enemy, crucify yourself and exalt Christ in your life. God gets all the glory because our weapons are not of this world, but of Him and His Holy Spirit.

This process works for any lie of the enemy, look at these comments ("You are not smart", "You are worthless", "You are a bad mother" etc.) or any stronghold (anger, jealously, lust, envy, etc.) that has built a giant strong tower in your mind. This is how you pull it down...brick by brick...you are delivered as you repeat the process so many times that it becomes as natural to you as breathing, it will become a way of life of victorious Christian living. This is why we must put on the helmet of salvation-to guard our thought-life, lest we allow the enemy to find a weakness in our armor and exploit it or lest we should memorize Scriptures that will be useful when the enemy comes against us to our specific weakness and point of vulnerability. Hold forth the shield of faith, draw the sword of the spirit and fight the good fight of faith.

Scriptures on the Power of Thoughts and Your Mind

Deuteronomy 30:19 I call heaven and earth to record this day against you, that I have set before you life and death, blessing and cursing: therefore choose life, that both thou and thy seed may live:

My Comment: For years, this verse haunted me. I didn't believe life — particularly love, joy, peace, etc. — were choices. I always thought circumstances played a role. Simply choosing love and joy was too easy. But what if it's true? Dr. Caroline Leaf says this in her book Switch On Your Brain, *"As we think, we change the physical nature of our brain. As we consciously direct our thinking, we can wire out toxic patterns of thinking and replace them with healthy thoughts."*

Romans 12:2 And be not conformed to this world: but be ye transformed by the renewing of your mind, that ye may prove what is that good, and acceptable, and perfect, will of God.

My Comment: Changing the way you think changes your perspective which changes how you act in the world. Paul's words aren't new. "Change your mind" is the central theme of Jesus' first sermon (Matt. 4:17).

Jesus challenged people to change their thinking because regardless how many times you read through the Bible, if your mind doesn't change, you will simply impose your biases and labels on the words you read.

2 Tim. 1: 7 For God hath not given us the spirit of fear; but of power, and of love, and of a sound mind.

My Comment: Basic fear says "If you jump off that cliff you won't make it. Get away from the cliff." This type of fear is healthy and good. But fear and distrust of life and people isn't from God, yet it seems hard-wired into our minds. We're afraid of being afraid. The Spirit always breathes love. When you choose fear, your life and legacy suffer.

Exodus 34:7 Keeping mercy for thousands, forgiving iniquity and transgression and sin, and that will by no means clear the guilty; visiting the iniquity of the fathers upon the children, and upon the children's children, unto the third and to the fourth generation.

My Comment: Another haunting verse here that speaks directly to the power of our thoughts. Not only do your thoughts shape your life. They also influence the lives of your future kids and their kids. Science has confirmed this truth. The science of epigenetics has shown that our dispositions, bad habits, anxiety, and hatred of cats can impact our kids even before they are conceived.

2 Corinthians 10:5 Casting down imaginations, and every high thing that exalteth itself against the knowledge of God, and bringing into captivity every thought to the obedience of Christ;

My Comment: Take every thought captive. What a great idea. But is it even possible? Well, if we trusted God's word, we would know it was possible. The answer to capturing your thoughts is right there in Scripture, hidden in plain sight.

Psalm 46:10 says, "Be still and know that I am God."

The powerful effects of prayer and meditation have been well-documented in recent years, again confirming what Christians should already know. Capturing your thoughts requires stillness, something most Americans, and many Christians, do not make time for. If we do not make time for prayer, our thoughts, emotions, and feelings will continue directing our lives.

Philippians 4:8 Finally, brethren, whatsoever things are true, whatsoever things are honest, whatsoever things are just, whatsoever things are pure, whatsoever things are lovely, whatsoever things are of good report; if there be any virtue, and if there be any praise, think on these things.

My Comment: Every now and then I meet someone who is different. You know the ones. These people see the world differently. They're calm. Nothing seems to shake them. They're almost impossible to offend, and they listen much more than they talk. They love everyone, even their enemies. Their joy and peace are infectious. When I encounter someone like this, I leave wondering what awesome sauce they take and where I can buy a jar. They truly leave behind the presence of the Lord.

People who are different understand Philippians 4:8. They choose love. They choose to see God's image in everyone. They choose well, and ruthlessly eliminate negativity. What you choose to see determines your reality. You have the power to change your reality by shifting your focus onto Jesus.

1 Corinthians 1:10 "Now I beseech you, brethren, by the name of our Lord Jesus Christ, that ye all speak the same thing, and that there be no divisions among you; but that ye be perfectly joined together in the same mind and in the same judgment."

My Comment: It is when we are united as believers in Christ that He commands His blessing. In Unity there is strength, safety, provision and blessing.

Personal Testimony of Casting Down Vain Imaginations

On the job there is always one person who for some reason tries to put us in a bad light. They question everything we do; expose any mistakes we might make. I have that at work. The more I dwelt on this person and their ways, especially as I was given a special assignment, the more guarded and anxious I found myself becoming.

The vain imaginations began to come, that they were out to undermine my talents and abilities and that I would fail in this project, the more that I dwelt on these thoughts, the more frustrated and anxious I became. You see, I had been through this before and was given a special project that was taken away because of people like this person and I found myself in a similar situation.

I did something different this time. I then began to seek the Lord about it and take authority over these vain imaginations. I sensed He was directing me to see them in another way, not as a threat but to listen to their questioning and use their comments to better prepare me for this special project. It has freed me to work more freely and confidently on this project, praise the Lord.

Practical Ways to Cast Down Vain Imaginations

- Think and dwell on good thoughts. Everything begins with

a thought.

- Remember this: Sow a thought, Reap an action. Sow an action, reap a character. Sow a character, reap a destiny.

- Develop a healthy mindset by reading the word daily, obeying the word.

- Pray against and don't dwell on vain imaginations.

- Mentally see yourself capturing that thought and casting it down in the name of Jesus.

- Believe, have faith, refuse thoughts of defeat, for faith pleases our Lord.

- See God as a Great God greater than any vain imagination, trial, test or negative feeling.

- Maintain a close association with men and women of faith and virtue as the scripture states iron sharpens iron.

- Don't dwell on negative feelings, do a positive action and those feelings will change, feelings always follow action.

- Keep your mind on the things of the Lord for He has promised to keep us in His peace.

- Choose to think and live in God's peace, love and joy not in the negative circumstances of life that come from time to time to all of us.

- Think about the good in people, especially our brothers and sisters in the faith not on their faults and shortcomings and love them, pray for them life can be a struggle and we are all on that same road called life.

- Keep yourself encouraged in the word of the Lord, let it fill and saturate your mind and thoughts, so you can be used by the Lord to be an encouragement to others.

- Remember our Heavenly Father made us and never think for one moment that your life is not important, it is important because you are important to God, so much that He sent His only begotten Son to die for you so that you might live a new life blessed by Him.

Conclusion

We all struggle with vain imaginations from time to time whose source is the enemy of our souls, satan. We have been given spiritual authority to cast these down through prayer and the word which is the sword of the spirit. If we will learn to cast down these vain imaginations and bring them into captivity to Christ authority, we will be more effective in our ministry for the Lord, in our relationships at church, at the workplace, home, wherever we go.

Vain imaginations are exactly what they are, vain and worthless, only the word of God is true and stands forever. Let's dwell, meditate and believe in His word so that when our work and life is over, we will leave a legacy for others to follow the truth of God's word. So, when vain imaginations come, remember our Heavenly Father made us, and never think for one moment that your life is not important. It is important because you are important to God, so much so that He sent His only begotten Son to die for you, that you might live a new life blessed by Him.

CHAPTER 25

Windows Of Opportunity In Life's Challenges

(JOHN 9:4)

Introduction

We all have been given a set measure of time. How we use that time and our windows of opportunities from God will either make for a purposeful life lived for God or a wasted life. Jesus said in John 9:4 — I must work the works of Him that sent me, while it is day; the night cometh when no man can work. In this lesson we will study the importance of living to do the works of God, despite persecution or ridicule and criticism.

Could it be that God had ordained the time of pandemic with COVID 19, persecution of the church and its followers, political debates, killing of the unborn, racial injustice and rioting, unemployment and other issues to serve as a window of opportunity for God through His church and His people to be glorified in the midst and that many turn to Him during these difficult times. As believers we need to ask ourselves, Lord, what do you want me to do during this window of opportunity?

Reading of John 9:1-41

(Summary of Story of the blind man healed)

In this story we see Jesus healing a man that was blind from birth. God had ordained this window of opportunity that the works of God should be made manifest in him and God would be glorified. Later we see the condemning attitude of the Pharisees toward Jesus because He healed the man on the Sabbath. There is a division in the crowd, some believed Jesus was from God and others said he was not of God because He did not observe the Sabbath.

After the Pharisees question the blind man, he tries to explain to them, but they expel him from the synagogue. Jesus' hearing of this event comes to the man He healed and asked if he believed in the son of God, and he agrees. Later Jesus confronts the Pharisees because they say they can see, but they're still in their sin because they refused to acknowledge Jesus as the Son of God.

Healing the Man Born Blind-
John 9:1-41

And as Jesus passed by, he saw a man which was blind from his birth. ² And his disciples asked him, saying, Master, who did sin, this man, or his parents, that he was born blind? ³ Jesus answered, Neither hath this man sinned, nor his parents: but that the works of God should be made manifest in him. ⁴ I must work the works of him that sent me, while it is day: the night cometh, when no man can work. ⁵ As long as I am in the world, I am the light of the world. ⁶ When he had thus spoken, he spat on the ground, and made clay of the spittle, and he anointed the eyes of the blind man with the clay, ⁷ And said unto him, Go, wash in the pool of Siloam, (which is by interpretation, Sent.) He went his way therefore, and washed, and came seeing. ⁸ The neighbours therefore, and they which before had seen him that he was blind, said, Is not this he that sat and begged? ⁹ Some said, This is he: others said, He is like him: but he said, I am he. ¹⁰ Therefore said they unto him, How were thine eyes opened? ¹¹ He answered and said, A man that is called Jesus made clay, and anointed mine eyes, and said unto me, Go to the pool of Siloam, and wash: and I went and washed, and I received sight. ¹² Then said they unto him, Where is he? He said, I know not.

Controversy Over the Man

¹³ They brought to the Pharisees him that aforetime was blind. ¹⁴ And it was the sabbath day when Jesus made the clay, and opened his eyes. ¹⁵ Then again the Pharisees also asked him how he had received his sight. He said unto them, He put clay upon mine eyes, and I washed, and do see. ¹⁶ Therefore said some of the Pharisees, This man is not of God, because he keepeth not the sabbath day. Others said, How can a man that is a sinner do such miracles? And there was a division among them. ¹⁷ They say unto the blind man again, What sayest thou of him, that he hath opened thine eyes? He said, He is a prophet. ¹⁸ But the Jews did not believe concerning him, that he had been blind, and received his sight, until they called the parents of him that had received his sight. ¹⁹ And they asked them, saying, Is this your son, who ye say was born blind? how then doth he now see? ²⁰ His parents answered them and said, We know that this is our son, and that he was born blind: ²¹ But by what means he now seeth, we know not; or who hath opened his eyes,

we know not: he is of age; ask him: he shall speak for himself. [22] These words spake his parents, because they feared the Jews: for the Jews had agreed already, that if any man did confess that he was Christ, he should be put out of the synagogue. [23] Therefore said his parents, He is of age; ask him. [24] Then again called they the man that was blind, and said unto him, Give God the praise: we know that this man is a sinner. [25] He answered and said, Whether he be a sinner or no, I know not: one thing I know, that, whereas I was blind, now I see. [26] Then said they to him again, What did he to thee? how opened he thine eyes? [27] He answered them, I have told you already, and ye did not hear: wherefore would ye hear it again? will ye also be his disciples? [28] Then they reviled him, and said, Thou art his disciple; but we are Moses' disciples. [29] We know that God spake unto Moses: as for this fellow, we know not from whence he is. [30] The man answered and said unto them, Why herein is a marvellous thing, that ye know not from whence he is, and yet he hath opened mine eyes. [31] Now we know that God heareth not sinners: but if any man be a worshipper of God, and doeth his will, him he heareth. [32] Since the world began was it not heard that any man opened the eyes of one that was born blind. [33] If this man were not of God, he could do nothing. [34] They answered and said unto him, Thou wast altogether born in sins, and dost thou teach us? And they cast him out.

Jesus Affirms His Deity

[35] Jesus heard that they had cast him out; and when he had found him, he said unto him, Dost thou believe on the Son of God? [36] He

answered and said, Who is he, Lord, that I might believe on him? [37] And Jesus said unto him, Thou hast both seen him, and it is he that talketh with thee. [38] And he said, Lord, I believe. And he worshipped him. [39] And Jesus said, For judgment I am come into this world, that they which see not might see; and that they which see might be made blind. [40] And some of the Pharisees which were with him heard these words, and said unto him, Are we blind also? [41] Jesus said unto them, If ye were blind, ye should have no sin: but now ye say, We see; therefore your sin remaineth.

Barnes Commentary

The works of him ... — The works of benevolence and mercy which God has commissioned me to do, and which are expressive of his goodness and power. This was on the Sabbath day John 9:14; and though Jesus had endangered his life (John 5:1-16) by working a similar miracle on the Sabbath, yet he knew that this was the will of God that he should do good, and that he would take care of his life.

While it is day — The day is the proper time for work — night is not. This is the general, the universal sentiment. While the day lasts it is proper to labor. The term "day" here refers to the life of Jesus, and to the opportunity thus afforded by working miracles. His life was drawing to a close. It was probably about six months after this when he was put to death. The meaning is, my life is near its close. While it continues, I must employ it in doing the works which God has appointed.

The night cometh — Night here represents death. It was drawing near, and he must therefore do what he had to do soon. It is not improbable, also, that this took place near the close of the Sabbath, as the sun was declining, and the shades of evening about to appear. This supposition will give increased beauty to the language which follows. No man can work — It is literally true that day is the appropriate time for toil, and that the night of death is a time when nothing can be done. Ecclesiastes 9:10.

Sharing Personal Experiences on doing God's work in a window of opportunity

In times past I worked as a volunteer as a speaker and counselor at Covenant House. It is a Catholic organization that provides shelter for young men and women who are homeless and need help. During this time the Lord had put it on my heart to do some work with young people. The church I attended at the time did not provide any opportunity and so I looked outside the four walls of the church. I went there every Monday night for two and a half years before the window of opportunity was closed. Many youths accepted the Lord; they witnessed the power of God answering prayer. Sometimes God opens windows of opportunities for a few moments in time or for years. Yet when He opens those windows, we need to take them in faith and understand it is only for a season.

Practical Applications on doing God's work during our window of opportunity of Life

- First, we must accept Jesus as Lord and Savior. The bible states in 2 Cor. 6:2 — now is the day of salvation. To work for God, we need to be born again.

- We must learn to be a disciple. A disciplined follower of Jesus is about learning of Him and being disciplined by Him, before we can do effective works led by His Spirit.

- Be willing to do the works that He has called us to, for which we may be criticized.

- Be willing to suffer for His name's sake, some believers may not accept us or we may be asked to leave a synagogue or church as the man who Jesus healed was put of the synagogue

- In this lesson we see working during the day as, while we have life, for the night which represents death, will one day come upon each of us and all our work for God will cease.

- God's word in Psalms 92:14 states that even in old age we will still bear fruit. We can work for God at any age, He does not discriminate and still provides windows of opportunities.

- God through Christ does His work in His own way, just as Jesus did when He spit on the ground made clay and put it on the man's eyes and told him to wash it off at a specific place. Some things He might ask of us may not fit into the norm of society but are we willing to do it despite criticisms we might receive.

- We need to be willing to pay the price for following Christ. During this time, we see Christians, even pastors put in jail in some states and churches being closed down for their beliefs. Yet God has raised up men and women who are bold in spirit and have led people to take the church outdoors, others are preaching and leading worship in some very difficult and dangerous areas where there has been rioting and chaos.

- Other pastors are not compromising and preaching truth from the pulpit risking their reputation and their lives. They are taking this window of opportunity to Glorify God and give honor and praise to Him who is the King of Kings and Lord of Lords who are willing to pay the price for the cause of Christ.

Conclusion

What is the Lord calling you to do for Him, is it to pray, fast, worship, preach, teach, witness, in dangerous areas, and feed the poor and needy. Are you willing to set aside time for Him to do those works for you. Are you willing to pay the price for your faith and respond to that window of opportunity the Lord is providing? There are a lot of needs in life, but He is calling us to specific works and specific needs and people.

Remember, He set aside His own life and died on a cross to redeem us from a life of sin and hell. I would like to share a quote — One life will soon be passed and what's done for Christ will last. Jesus said in John 9:4 — I must work the works of him that sent me, while it is day: the night cometh, when no man can work. Let us not miss this window of opportunity that God has given us during this critical time in our nation to praise and glorify Him and work for Him so that others may come to know our Lord and His salvation.

About The Author

Just a short bio of my life's accomplishments. I hold a Bachelor of Arts degree in Theology. Former Member of Toastmasters International. High School teacher in earlier years. Worked in Government for 30 years. Taught Sunday School to both young and older adults for several years. Did volunteer work at Covenant House with youth as both a speaker and counselor. Involved in different aspects of church ministry, including men's ministry, youth ministry, holding Bible studies, street ministry and leading a Connect group of adults as part of the church's ministry of connecting members to one another in small group settings. Presently work for 911 as a Database Specialist and Phone communications. It's a job with the purpose of saving lives and so it is the work of the Lord, for which I am passionate and eternally grateful.

Bibliography

Quote from NFL star Danny "DJ" Ware (Chapter titled, Are You at the Breaking Point in Your Life). Reference from Our Daily Bread

Quotes from Elizabeth Keckley and Joshua Wolf Shenk (Chapter titled, Scriptures to Fight Depression and Hopelessness)

Quote from Monica Araya (Chapter titled, Jesus our Hope in a Hopeless World)

Quote from Ronald F. Youngblood, (Chapter titled, The Importance of Not Losing Our Joy)

Quote from Rick Warren, Pastor of Saddleback Church, (Chapter titled, In our Weakness He is Made Strong)

Commentaries used are from Matthew Henry, Benson Commentary and Barnes Commentary

Greek definitions are taken from Online Bible Hub

Quotes from James Merritt (Chapter titled, Jesus Our Crisis Manager)

Quote from Roxane Cohen Silver, PhD, the University of California, Irvine, psychologist, (Chapter titled, God Has A Purpose For Allowing Adversity in our Lives)

Statistics From SingleCare Team (2024) *Stress statistics 2024: How common is stress, and who's most affected. Updated Nov. 4, 2024*

Quote from Glen Ryswyk, An Assemblies of God chaplain and clinical director, (Chapter titled, Overcoming Stress God's Way)

Quote from G.K. Chesterton, (Chapter titled, Returning To Our First Love)

Quote from Dr. Billy Graham, (Chapter titled, Spiritual Warfare)

Quote from John Hagee, (Chapter titled, Spiritual Warfare)

www.ingramcontent.com/pod-product-compliance
Lightning Source LLC
Chambersburg PA
CBHW031513120626
46545CB00005B/1864